Games, Ideas and Activities for Primary Poetry

Games, Ideas and Activities for Primary Poetry

Virginia Bower

Longman
is an imprint of

Harlow, England • London • New York • Boston • San Francisco • Toronto • Sydney • Singapore • Hong Kong
Tokyo • Seoul • Taipei • New Delhi • Cape Town • Madrid • Mexico City • Amsterdam • Munich • Paris • Milan

PEARSON EDUCATION LIMITED
Edinburgh Gate
Harlow CM20 2JE
United Kingdom
Tel: +44 (0)1279 623623
Fax: +44 (0)1279 431059
Website: www.pearsoned.co.uk

First edition published in Great Britain in 2011

© Pearson Education Limited 2011

The right of Virginia Bower to be identified as author of this work has been asserted by her in accordance with the Copyright, Designs and Patents Act 1988.

Pearson Education is not responsible for the content of third party internet sites.

ISBN: 978-1-4082-5934-4

British Library Cataloguing in Publication Data
A CIP catalogue record for this book can be obtained from the British Library

Library of Congress Cataloging in Publication Data

Bower, Virginia.
  Games, ideas and activities for primary poetry / Virginia Bower.
      p. cm.
  Includes bibliographical references and index.
  ISBN 978-1-4082-5934-4 (pbk. : alk. paper) 1. Poetry—Study and teaching (Elementary) 2. Language arts (Elementary) 3. Education, Elementary—Activity programs. I. Title.
  LB1575.B619 2011
  372.64'044—dc22   2010054137

10 9 8 7 6 5 4 3 2 1
15 14 13 12 11

Typeset in 8.5/12 NewsGoth BT by 73
Printed in Malaysia (CTP-V P)

This book is dedicated to my mum and dad to whom I owe a love of reading and a love of learning, and to Peter for the limericks and the laughs! Thanks to you all.

Contents

Chapter 5 - Senses and feelings   130

Chapter 6 - Poetic forms   162

Chapter 7 - Poetry all around us   195

Chapter 8 - Ideas to promote talk in the classroom   227

Introduction

Purpose of the book

To introduce this book I would like to begin with a quote from Michael Rosen:

What poetry offers is the possibility that language can be used for entirely different purposes: to affect people through the play of language; to enable the writer, through the act of writing, to discover something about herself; to enable a community of writers, like a class, or a school, to create a shared set of understandings; to enable individuals and groups to discover in each other different and valid experiences and identities. *(Michael Rosen, 1997)*

Rosen's words summarise for me why the teaching of poetry is a vital component of primary classroom life and why, as teachers, we need to become confident and knowledgeable with this genre. Within this quote alone, Rosen identifies some of the key themes that this Classroom Gem aims to explore, through its practical ideas for activities relating to poetry across Key Stage 1 and Key Stage 2. He implies that poetry has an implicit power; the power to use language for your own purposes, to create particular and unique effects. He states that a reader or a writer of poetry is able to find out more about themselves through this medium and about the people and world around them, developing and shaping an identity and recognising that experiences can be shared with mutual benefits.

It is through poetry that a teacher can become more acquainted with their pupils' likes and dislikes, what makes them laugh, how they feel about the world around them. In this way, by tapping into their existing knowledge and understanding of the world, a closer relationship is formed and the teacher is able to use his or her findings to engage and motivate the children across the curriculum. The great thing about studying and enjoying poetry is that there are no 'right' or 'wrong' answers. Poetry is personal – what *you* think, what *you* like/dislike, what *you* take from this literary form – that is what is important and this has the potential to set children free from some of the more prescriptive aspects of the primary curriculum. This personal element also makes poetry incredibly inclusive. Whether children are reading poems to themselves or aloud, listening to poets reading their poetry, or writing their own poems from their own experiences of life or for a particular audience, they can enjoy the genre at their own level because there are no rights or wrongs.

I feel very strongly that *all* children should have the opportunity to enjoy a wide range of poetry and have tried, therefore, to structure the games, ideas and activities so that they are adaptable for all abilities. Although some of the activities are key stage specific, this is often because the poem or poems that have been used within the activity are more appropriate for a particular age group. Differentiation is central to good classroom practice, but I have avoided identifying activities for specific groups of children as I am sure that all teachers are able to modify and adapt where necessary to accommodate all the children in their class. I have, however, tried to make full use of speaking and listening, drama and role play, as well as reading and writing, so that users of this book should find plenty of ideas to engage and motivate all their pupils, whatever their level of knowledge and understanding.

Structure of the book

The book is divided into ten chapters under the following headings:

- Narrative poetry
- Poetry to perform
- Humorous poetry and word play
- Poetry for all occasions
- Senses and feelings
- Poetic forms
- Poetry all around us
- Ideas to promote talk in the classroom
- Ideas to promote reading in the classroom
- Ideas to promote writing in the classroom

Each chapter has an introduction that includes a brief discussion of the theme and an outline of the chapter structure. Each activity within the chapter has a title that gives a clue to the activity itself and then a brief introduction. You are then told for which key stage the activity is most suited (this is, however, very flexible and you may well find that you can adapt a KS1 activity for your KS2 class or vice versa); then the aims of the activity (many of which are directly linked to National Curriculum objectives) are described, followed by the resources you will need. The resources section is key to each activity, as it has been designed to reduce your workload. Locating resources can be a very time-consuming practice and can sometimes hinder classroom practitioners. I have, therefore, provided the poem(s) needed for nearly all the activities in the book, either within the appendices or within a web link that takes you directly to a copy of the poem(s), or I have written a poem specifically for the activity. Very occasionally, where a poem is not available in any of these three ways, I have signposted to a particular anthology that most schools would probably have anyway. I have made every effort to use a wide range of poems and poets from old classics to modern verses; from serious to humorous; from lengthy to very brief; and from well known to obscure. In this way I hope that everyone – adults and children – will find many poems they can enjoy.

After the resources section, the activities are described in the 'What to do' section. This is followed, in many activities, by 'Variations', which offer some alternative ideas linked to the main activity. Finally, where suitable, there are some suggestions for cross-curricular links. The aim of each activity is to promote confidence in both teachers and pupils, so that they are able to share, enjoy and learn together. Many student teachers and experienced classroom practitioners have said to me that they shy away from teaching poetry, either because of their own negative experiences of poetry when they were themselves young learners, or because of a perceived lack of subject knowledge. This book aims to dispel some of these concerns and actively promotes the idea that poetry is accessible to all and has much to offer every one of us.

After the activities, I have included an appendix that contains poems, links to websites, a range of resources and ideas, and a glossary of terms.

A few tips

Although the book is structured to cover a different theme in each chapter, you will find many overlaps. For example, many narrative poems make fantastic performance poems and most of the activities in the book could have been included in the chapter promoting ideas for talk. You can, therefore, use the book flexibly, dipping in to chapters and adapting activities to suit your needs. Another useful tip when using this book and accessing poetry online is to set up a YouTube converter. YouTube has an amazing range of resources and you can find clips of poets performing their poems and a wealth of other video material to support you with teaching poetry. If you find, however, that you cannot access YouTube in school, you need to download a YouTube converter. Go to www. dvdvideosoft.com and click on 'Free YouTube Download'. Once you have downloaded the program, you will have an icon on your desktop to open it. Once you find a video you want to use, copy the URL of the video, the converter tells you where to paste it, then click on download and it will be saved to your documents (thanks to Becky – one of my ex-students – for this helpful advice).

Finally, my last tip is just to say 'Go for it!' Immerse yourself and your class in poetry and then sit back and enjoy the fantastic discussions, role plays, displays, books and writing that will emerge from this wonderful genre. Good luck!

Acknowledgements

I would like to thank Peter for his support, encouragement and, most importantly, his insightful contributions.

I would also like to thank my colleagues at Canterbury Christ Church University who have offered up their favourite poems and have supported me with friendship, ideas and coffee.

Publisher's acknowledgements

We are grateful to the following for permission to reproduce copyright material:

The Trustees of Walter de la Mare and the Society of Authors as their representative for 'Someone', 'The Cupboard' and 'The Rainbow' by Walter de la Mare; Faber and Faber Ltd for 'Prelude 1' by TS Eliot from *Complete Poems and Plays of TS Eliot*, Faber & Faber 2004.

In some instances we have been unable to trace the owners of copyright material, and we would appreciate any information that would enable us to do so.

Chapter 1
Narrative poetry

Introduction

Narrative poems are poems that tell a story. They can be long and rambling, going into great depth about the event they are describing; or they can be fairly short and snappy, briefly describing something that has happened, from one person's perspective. By their very nature, narrative poems are often incredibly atmospheric and therefore best read aloud. It is important to practise this art before you read aloud to the children, ensuring that you are familiar with the rhythms and language structure of the poem you are going to use, so that you can give the best possible recital, drawing the children in and immersing them in the atmosphere of the poem. Finding recordings of narrative poems being recited – perhaps by the original poet or by an actor – is another way of presenting to the children and allows you to sit back and enjoy.

Some of the most popular narrative poems are based around historical events. This is an excellent, natural link with history and can help to bring the era/event/personalities alive for the children. Narrative poems can support children's understanding of a moment in time and they can be encouraged to think about the reliability of historical sources, focusing on perspective and bias, truth and opinion. By comparing evidence from a range of sources – tales and myths, poems, non-fiction 'fact' books, letters and diaries etc. – children can begin to make their own judgements and become more critical learners.

Narrative poetry makes the perfect starting point for drama and role play and children can begin to understand more about the characters involved through activities such as hot-seating, conscience corridor, thought-tracking and freeze frames (see Appendix 2). This can lead on to the creation of character profiles and setting descriptions and strong links can be made between narrative, poetry and non-fiction.

Through studying narrative poems, children begin to realise that they all have stories to tell and that they can tell them through this genre. Their narratives might be centred around exciting events in their lives, for example the holiday of a lifetime or the birth of a sibling, or they might just be about something that happened in school or when they were at the park at the weekend. In this way, all children in the class can be included and can be encouraged to find their 'voice' through narrative poetry.

The chapter has five ideas suitable for both KS1 and KS2, five more relevant to KS1 and five for KS2. Remember, however, that this is just a guide and it is worth having a look at all the activities and the poems recommended as you may find something that works particularly well with a topic you are studying.

Chocoholics delight

This activity introduces children to the idea that poems can tell stories and that they can have a structure much like a story, with a clear beginning, middle and end. It introduces the idea that a poem can consist merely of retelling an event.

Suitable for

KS1
KS2

Aims

- To recognise that poems can tell stories.
- To use drama to retell a narrative poem.

Resources

- 'Chocolate Cake' by Michael Rosen: www.poemhunter.com/poem/chocolate-cake/

What to do

1. Read 'Chocolate Cake' by Michael Rosen. Make sure that the poem is read with plenty of expression and actions (each time I read this poem to a class I try to improve my own performance, adding more expression, actions, accents etc). It would be a great idea to have a real chocolate cake to use whilst reading and then perhaps to share it afterwards.
2. How do we know this is a narrative poem? In groups or as a class, retell the story, focusing on the key points. Draw a story 'mountain' on the board and ask individuals to come up and write a few words on the mountain that would help someone to retell the narrative poem.

3. Divide the poem into four sections – when the boy awakes and feels hungry; creeping down to the kitchen; eating the cake; the next day. Divide the class into four groups and ask each group to develop a freeze frame (see Appendix 2) to represent their part of the poem.
4. Reread the poem and as each group hears their section of the poem, they move into their freeze frame.
5. Once the poem is finished, pupils could discuss an incident in their own lives that might be turned into a narrative poem. This could be followed up in a future lesson.

Variations

Instead of freeze frames, pupils could act out a scene of the poem, focusing on representing the key events in the narrative. Alternatively, the teacher might engage the children in thought-tracking (see Appendix 2). This is a good way to immerse the children in the narrative and can lead to some excellent writing.

Cross-curricular link

PSHE – have you ever been tempted to do something that you know is wrong? How did you feel before/during/after?

A dark, dark poem

Because of the storytelling nature of narrative poetry, it is sometimes useful to use a picture book or short story as the stimulus for writing a narrative poem. This activity uses the text 'A Dark, Dark Tale' by Ruth Brown.

Suitable for

KS1
KS2

Aims

* To use a picture book as the stimulus for writing a narrative poem.

Resources

* 'A Dark, Dark Tale' by Ruth Brown

What to do

1. Read 'A Dark, Dark Tale', giving the children plenty of time to look at the wonderful illustrations. Before you read the last page, ask the children to predict what is in the box. Discuss the language and how suspense is built up. Reread, asking pupils to join in with the words 'dark, dark' on each page.
2. If the story was a poem, what would it look like set out on the page? Rewrite the first few pages as lines of a poem. Note how the repetition forms a pattern throughout. What effect does this have?
3. Working together as a class (shared writing), rewrite the story, as a poem, using different settings, e.g.

   Once upon a time there was
   A dark, dark forest.

> *In the forest there was*
> *A dark, dark castle.*
>
> 4. Discuss whether there are other picture books that the children feel could be used as a stimulus for narrative poetry.

Variations

- KS2 children could be challenged further by thinking about how they might change the adjectives 'dark, dark' (e.g. 'a spooky, spooky tale') and how this changes the mood and atmosphere of the poem.
- All children could be encouraged to produce illustrations for the class poem, using the wonderful pictures in the original as a stimulus for their own ideas.

Cross-curricular link

Art – the use of colour, shading, tone etc. to portray mood and atmosphere.

Someone came knocking

It is important that children realise narrative poems can be short and do not necessarily have to tell a long, complicated tale. This will encourage them to think about events in their own lives and how these could be used to create a poem.

Suitable for

KS1
KS2

Aims

- To demonstrate how small events can be used to create a narrative poem.

Resources

- 'Some One' by Walter de la Mare (Appendix 1a)

What to do

1. Tell the children a story about your life, where something odd/mysterious/spooky has happened. In groups, ask the children to share any stories that they have about incidents in their lives along the same theme. Feed back to the class.
2. Explain that sometimes poets write narrative poems about strange things that have happened to them or that they have heard about. Read 'Some One' by Walter de la Mare. Discuss the main event of the poem – opening a door and finding no one there. This is a very minor event, and yet the poet has written an effective, atmospheric poem – how has he achieved his effect? You could discuss rhyme, rhythm, wonderful vocabulary etc.
3. Ask the children to think of questions that they would like to ask the poet if he were still alive. Return to one of the stories that a child told at the beginning of the session about an incident in their own

lives. Encourage other members of the class to ask questions, gathering more information and details about the incident. Record these on the board.

4. Explain that if you are going to write a narrative poem about an event in your own life, it is useful to start with an outline of the story and then think about the questions people might ask to 'fill in the gaps'. These details might then provide additional vocabulary, which you could use in your own narrative poem.

Variations

- This poem by Walter de la Mare would make a wonderful performance poem, with the children acting out and including sound effects. It is a very easy poem to learn because of the rhythm and rhyme, so all children could take part and join in. This would make an excellent performance for an assembly to the rest of the school.

Cross-curricular link

ICT – if children were to perform this poem, it could be recorded and become part of a collection of electronic resources for the whole school. Children could evaluate their own performances and consider how they might improve for the next time.

Cowardly, cowardly custard

This activity is based on the light-hearted narrative poem 'The Tale of Custard the Dragon'. It contains some very colourful descriptions, which can be used to fire up children's imaginations.

Suitable for

KS1
KS2

Aims

- To create imaginary worlds and characters.

Resources

- 'The Tale of Custard the Dragon' by Ogden Nash: www.eecs.harvard.edu/~keith/poems/Custard.html

What to do

1. Read 'The Tale of Custard the Dragon' by Ogden Nash. Do the children like the fact that it is a more light-hearted narrative poem, with strange creatures as the main characters and unusual events occurring?
2. If you have confident readers in the class, give volunteers a verse each to read aloud. Ask the rest of the class to make a mental note of their favourite character from the poem and try to remember how that character is described, as the poem is read again.
3. Go through the characters who appear in the poem and discuss how the poet describes them. Look at specific features such as similes – 'Belinda was as brave as a barrelful of bears' – and made-up words such as 'realio' and 'trulio'.

4. Return to the first verse, which describes where and with whom Belinda lives. Explain to the children that they are going to create an imaginary place where they would like to live and some imaginary creatures with whom they would like to share this dwelling. They can record the place and inhabitants in any way they like – through a picture/cartoon/written description/poem.
5. Share their ideas with the class.

Variations

• Children could have great fun performing this poem, perhaps making masks to enhance the performance and using musical instruments for sound effects.

Cross-curricular link

Art and DT – making masks and props either to match the characters in the original poem or to go with their own imaginary creatures.

Poems from memories

This activity needs no resources or props, or even any poems! Children just need their memories . . .

Suitable for

KS1
KS2

Aims

- To include relevant detail when writing poems.

Resources

- Just a memory

What to do

1. Think of a theme that you know will be relevant to the children in your class. A useful one to start with is 'food'. Ask the children to close their eyes and to think of a memory that involves food. This might be when they tried something for the first time and loved/hated it; a birthday party with a wonderful cake; a meal in a very special restaurant; eating in a foreign country; or being forced to eat sprouts! Give them a few minutes to think of a memory.

2. Ask them to imagine that they are back in that time and place. Tell them you are going to ask them a series of questions and they are going to jot down the answers (this can be in writing or pictures). Ask the following questions:

   - What can you see?
   - What can you smell?
   - What can you hear?
   - How are you feeling?

3. Model how the answers to these questions can be turned into a narrative poem. For example:

I am sitting in a café at the edge of the sea
My eyes are filled with the shimmering light glinting off the waves
The saltiness of the air fills my nose and grilled fish wafts on the breeze
I hear the clattering of pans; the low murmur of holiday makers' voices
I am relaxed, at peace; my tummy rumbles
At last! My meal arrives
Ah! Satisfaction!

By Virginia Bower

4. Use the ideas of one of the children and write a poem altogether from these ideas.
5. If there is time, the children can use their memories to write their own narrative poems.

Variations

- You can develop an excellent class collection of narrative poems using this method and different themes. Because you are relying merely on the children's memories, you should never run out of material.

Cross-curricular link

History – narrative poems written from memories are closely linked with history, and children can be encouraged in this way to think about their own and their families' histories.

Poor Dad!

This is an activity for younger children, to introduce them to the idea that a narrative poem can tell a very ordinary, familiar – and funny! – tale.

Suitable for

KS1

Aims

- To raise awareness that people's own experiences can be used to create poems.

Resources

- 'Dad and the Cat and the Tree' by Kit Wright: http://mybroadband.co.za/vb/ showthread.php?55830-Your-Favourite-Poem/page3

What to do

1. Ask the class if any of them has a cat and, if so, whether they have any funny stories about their cat. Share these with the rest of the class. Are there any cats in stories or on the television that are clever or naughty or funny?
2. Explain to the children that sometimes people write poems about their cats or their families or events in their lives. Read 'Dad and the Cat and the Tree' by Kit Wright. Give the children some time to talk in pairs about the events of the poem.
3. Reread the poem and then ask the children to retell the events of the poem. Why do you think the poet wrote about these events? Do you think he based them on real events in his life? What is this poem doing? – telling a story.
4. Return to one of the stories that the children told earlier. How might we turn this into a poem? Ask the child to slowly retell the story

> and, as they do so, begin to write out the events in the style of a poem. Explain to the children that although Kit Wright's poem rhymed, ours does not have to – it just needs to tell the story. Read the poem to the children.

Variations

- It would be great fun to use this poem as a starting point for looking at how stories can be told in different ways. The children could be encouraged to present their own stories in a way that suits them – perhaps as a dramatic scene, a story board, a piece of art work or, indeed, a poem.

Cross-curricular link

Music – the children could tell their story through sound, using different instruments to represent the events. Alternatively, you could read the Kit Wright poem and encourage the children to think of a suitable musical accompaniment as the various disasters occur.

There was a little girl

Children may well be familiar with the first verse of the poem used in this activity. However, the next two verses are not well known and they change a simple nursery rhyme into an interesting narrative poem.

Suitable for

KS1

Aims

- To ask questions to clarify understanding.
- To make predictions.

Resources

- 'Jemima' by Henry Wadsworth Longfellow (Appendix 1b)

What to do

1. Ask the children if they know the rhyme that starts, 'There was a little girl who had a little curl'. If they do, ask them to recite it. If they have not heard of these first lines, read the first verse to them. It is likely that they will be familiar with the first verse of this poem. Explain that this first verse is only part of a whole poem that tells a story.
2. What do you think the story might be about? How do you think the poem might continue? When she is good, what good deeds might she do? When she is naughty, what bad deeds might she do?
3. Read the other two verses of the poem. Ask the children to explain in their own words what Jemima did that was so naughty, and what her punishment was. There are words and phrases in the poem that the children may not have understood – 'truckle bed', 'hurraying with her heels', 'emphatic' – and this may limit their understanding of

what has happened in the poem. Encourage them to formulate questions to aid their understanding.
4. Reread the poem so that the children are able to listen to the words again and connect their new understanding to the unfamiliar words.

Variations

- This would make a great performance poem – I am sure the children would enjoy playing the part of naughty Jemima!

Stories of old women

This activity uses rhymes that children will be familiar with and therefore they provide a good context for supporting children with sequencing events and recounting accurately.

Suitable for

KS1

Aims

- To sequence events and recount them accurately.

Resources

- 'There Was an Old Woman Who Lived in a Shoe': www.allaboutmammals. com/paint/rhymes/coloring/Oldladyshoe.shtml
- 'There Was an Old Lady': www.rhymes.org.uk/there_was_an_old_lady.htm

What to do

1. Who knows any poems or songs about old ladies? Give children time to talk in pairs and discuss any ideas they have.
2. Read the first line of 'There Was an Old Woman Who Lived in a Shoe' and see if the children can continue the rhyme. Read the whole rhyme and discuss any words that might be unfamiliar, e.g. 'broth' and 'soundly'. This is a narrative poem, because it tells a short story. Can you retell this story in your own words? Have a go at this as a class, creating a flow chart on the board, summarising the key points.
3. Read the first line of 'There Was an Old Lady'. Does anyone know how this continues? Have a go at singing this as a class (it would be useful to have visual prompts of all the creatures she swallows).
4. Each group in the class produces a drawing to represent a part of the poem, so that you end up with a story board showing the sequence of events. These can be used as prompts when the children sing or recite the poem, helping them with the order of events.

Variations

- On the first website above, there is a lovely activity where the children can use a piece of software that allows them to colour in a picture of the old woman who lived in a shoe. This could be an extension activity or could be built into an ICT lesson.

Cross-curricular link

ICT – see Variations above.

A fine romance

'The Owl and the Pussy-Cat' is a classic narrative poem. It has a wonderful rhythm and cadence and plenty of opportunities for children to join in.

Suitable for

KS1

Aims

* To identify the effect of rhythm in a poem.

Resources

* 'The Owl and the Pussy-Cat' by Edward Lear: www.nonsenselit.org/Lear/ns/pussy.html

What to do

1. Tell the children that you are going to read them a story poem about a romance between an owl and a cat. Ask them to close their eyes and listen to the rhythm of the poem as you read it. Try to really exaggerate the rhythm as you read it aloud.
2. Read the poem again, identifying any words that the children may not have heard before, e.g. 'quince' and 'runcible' (it is not vital that children understand every word of a poem, but they may be curious).
3. Have the poem up on the board so that the children can see it. Point out the last three lines in each stanza – how they repeat the fourth to last line. Ask them to join in with these lines as you read the poem again, and encourage them to keep to the speed and rhythm that you are following.
4. What sort of atmosphere does the rhythm create in this story poem? How does it help the story? A strong rhythm often carries the story along, and with this type of 'sing-song' rhythm it is quite relaxing, as if you were bobbing along on a boat.

Variations

- Because of the persistent rhythms and refrains of Edward Lear's poems, they are a great choice for encouraging children to learn 'off by heart' and then recite. 'The Owl and the Pussy-Cat' would be a wonderful poem to learn and share with other classes.

Sausage mayhem

Many narrative poems are, by their nature, quite long. This activity, however, uses a short, fun, compact poem that children can learn and recite.

Suitable for

KS1

Aims

- To speak with clear diction.

Resources

- 'Whoever Sausage a Thing' (anonymous; Appendix 1c)

What to do

1. Tell the children that you are going to read them a story poem about sausages (that should make them laugh before you even begin!).
2. Read the poem – try to use a sing-song voice, picking up on the regular rhythm and rhyme of the poem (this will help the children to memorise the lines).
3. Reread the poem, encouraging the children to join in if they remember any words or lines. Ask a volunteer to retell the story in their own words and write bullet points on the board of the main details as they do so. This will act as a memory prompt as the children begin to learn the poem.
4. Ask for six volunteers (including preferably three who can whistle). Explain that when you reread the poem, those that can whistle will whistle a little tune at the appropriate moment; then, when dancing is mentioned, all six will dance around the room. Again, these actions will help the children to memorise the poem. Read the poem with the children performing.

5. Explain to the children that when we are reciting a poem, it is important to speak very clearly so that everyone is able to hear. Practise each line at a time with the whole class, building up to a recital of the whole poem.

Variations

- This would make a great performance poem. Children could work in groups, taking on the roles of boy, shopkeeper and sausages.

Cross-curricular link

Drama – speaking clearly; taking on roles.

The fate of the knight

In this activity the children will read the poem 'Death and the Knight' by Tony Mitton and will explore the incredible atmosphere the poet creates.

Suitable for

KS2

Aims

* To identify how a poet creates a particular atmosphere.

Resources

* 'Death and the Knight' by Tony Mitton: www.tonymitton.co.uk/#/death-and-the-knight/4534268843

What to do

1. Go to the web page listed above and you will find the poem. There is also a short comment after the poem by Tony Mitton, explaining how Death was represented in the Middle Ages. Read this to the children before you read the poem.
2. Have the web page showing on the board so that the children can see how the poet has used a particular font to present his poem, setting the scene effectively within a particular historical era. Read the poem to the class, ensuring that you read slowly and clearly, putting plenty of expression into your voice. This is a particularly atmospheric poem and children need time to soak up the wonderful language and rhythm.
3. Discuss the poem – what do the children think of it? Begin to analyse the poet's superb use of language and the effect this has, e.g. 'torn at the Turk', 'his words blew dry as the dust where it drifts on the ground'. How does the use of language engage the reader with this narrative poem?

4. Reread the poem, asking the children to focus on the rhythm and rhyme. What effect does this have?
5. If there is time, the children could create a story board, representing the different scenes in the poem.

Variations

- This would make a wonderful poem to perform. The regular rhythm and rhyme make it an easy poem to memorise and the children could make masks and props for their performance.

Cross-curricular link

History – looking at customs and traditions from different ages.

A spooky tale

This activity uses the poem 'Flannan Isle' by Wilfrid Wilson Gibson. It is a fantastic, atmospheric poem and the children will begin to understand how effective poetry can be in creating mood and tension.

Suitable for

KS2

Aims

- To identify key words that create atmosphere and mood.

Resources

- 'Flannan Isle' by Wilfrid Wilson Gibson: www.poetry-archive.com/g/flannan_isle.html, www.snapsandbytes.co.uk/poem.html and www.bbc.co.uk/dna/h2g2/A1061335

What to do

1. Read the historical story of Flannan Isle at www.bbc.co.uk/dna/h2g2/A1061335. Then access www.snapsandbytes.co.uk/poem.html, where you will find a script of the poem with accompanying sound effects. Read the poem to the children.
2. Give the children plenty of time to discuss both the story and the narrative poem and ask them which they preferred and why.
3. Reread the poem, asking the children to note down any words they hear that seem to promote a sinister, spooky atmosphere. After rereading, gather their ideas and write down any key words on the board. Discuss why the poet has used these words, and the impact they have on the reader.
4. Give the children copies of the poem, and ask them to work in groups, reading a verse each, and recording any other words that

they feel are 'atmospheric'. These can then be added to the main list on the board. This list can later be printed off and each child can have a copy to stick into their writing journals/literacy books to be used at a future time to help them with their own atmospheric writing.

Variations

- This would be a wonderful poem to perform, and I nearly put this idea into Chapter 2. It lends itself beautifully to drama and role play – thought-tracking, hot-seating, freeze frames etc. (see Appendix 2).

Cross-curricular link

History – this poem could promote a discussion about the reliability of the printed word. 'Flannan Isle' is apparently not historically accurate, although it is based on a real life event. We need to encourage our children to be critical, questioning readers; by introducing them to two different versions of an historical event, we are giving them the opportunity to explore and investigate the validity of texts to which they are exposed.

A moral for us all

There's nothing like a story with a good, strong moral at the end. Many poems are based on morals and this activity uses a real classic.

Suitable for

KS2

Aims

● To use knowledge of other texts you have read.

Resources

● 'Jim' by Hillaire Belloc: www.theotherpages.org/poems/belloc01.html
● Stories/fables with morals: www.aesops-fables.org.uk/aesop-fable-the-lion-and-the-mouse.htm

What to do

1. Many stories have a moral – ask the children if they can think of any. What about 'The Hare and the Tortoise'? What is the moral here?
2. Read 'Jim' by Hillaire Belloc. What is the moral of this story?
3. Using the second website above, read some of Aesop's fables. Identify the moral in each.
4. Choose a favourite fable and reread this, identifying the moral. As a class, write a four-line poem that encompasses this moral, e.g. for 'The Hare and the Tortoise' you could have:

So listen all you speedy chaps
A little wisdom is perhaps
More useful than long legs that pace
As brains can help you win a race!
　　　　　　By Virginia Bower

5. If the children feel confident, they could have a go at this themselves, choosing a suitable fable, identifying the moral and writing two or three couplets. These could be displayed alongside the original fables on the wall with suitable illustrations.

Variations

- It would be good fun to explore in more depth the 'Cautionary Tales for Children' by Hillaire Belloc. They make great reading (although quite gruesome!) and you could create story boards/cartoons/illustrations from these wonderful poems.

Cross-curricular link

PSHE – understanding that your own actions can have an effect on others.

A biblical tale

Often narrative poems are based on a well-known event taken from sources such as the Bible, myths, legends etc. Making links between stories and poems can help children with their own poetry writing.

Suitable for

KS2

Aims

- To identify sources of inspiration for poetry writing.

Resources

- 'Noah' by Roy Daniells: www.stitcherymall.com/pipermail/biblemat/2005-December/002884.html
- The Bible
- Greek myths and legends
- Historical tales

What to do

1. Talk to the class about narrative poems and how they are often based on real life or imaginary events. Can they think of any examples?
2. Read 'Noah' by Roy Daniells. What is this poem about? Where has the poet got his inspiration from? Has he told the whole story in this one poem? The poet has taken a story from the Bible and has imagined how it might have been with Noah trying to persuade people that they needed to join him on the Ark. He has imagined what it must have been like to have seen the people drowning because they did not believe that the Flood would happen.
3. Ask the children to discuss in their groups any stories that they remember from different subjects they have studied, e.g. Greek

myths and legends/tales of Henry VIII/other Bible stories/tales from other countries and cultures. Feed back to the whole class and make a list on the board.

4. Take one example and discuss how this might be made into a poem. You need to consider the key details and the perspective from which you wish to write the poem. Who will be telling the story? Will it be Henry VIII, or one of his wives, or the executioner, or a small boy who watches the royal procession?

5. Give the children time to choose a favourite story and then begin to make notes about how this might be presented as a poem, thinking about key words and the effect they want to have on the reader. If there is enough time, the children could begin writing their poems, but this should not be rushed and they may wish to do some research before attempting writing.

Variations

- If you have access to the ICT suite, the children could research some of their favourite historical/Biblical stories and begin to gather information that they could use at a later date to write poems linked with a story.

Cross-curricular link

History and religious education – turning historical and religious events into poems is an excellent way of exploring episodes and experiences from different perspectives.

Chasing dreams

Often narrative poems are about quests – people trying to find hidden treasure, the answer to the unknown, or fame and fortune. The language used to describe the hardships encountered is an important feature for children to analyse.

Suitable for

KS2

Aims

- To identify features of language used for a specific purpose.

Resources

- 'Legend' by Judith Wright: www.tamborine-mtn-u3a.com/page14.html

What to do

1. Read 'Legend' by Judith Wright. What is this narrative poem about? It is a quest poem – the blacksmith's boy is searching for his dream and has to strive through adverse conditions and hardships to reach his goal.
2. How does the poet achieve her effects? What devices does she use? Reread the poem, with the children picking out any effective methods used, e.g. there is a great deal of personification in the poem – 'cobwebs snatched', 'mountains jumped' and the night was ready to 'swallow him' – and many similes – 'ran like a hare', 'climbed like a fox'. What effect do these features have?
3. Imagine you are going on a quest – to find knowledge or treasure or a person. Ask the children to invent three hazards that they will have to battle through on their journey and then describe how these hazards were overcome. Model a scenario, e.g. 'You have to cross a raging torrent, with dangerously sharp rocks hidden beneath the roaring

water. You find a very long branch from a tree and, using this as a pole vault, you launch yourself, like a leaping gazelle, from one river bank to the other avoiding death by millimetres.'

4. Give the children time to come up with their own hazards and solutions, encouraging them to use powerful language; they can record these either through writing or through mini story boards.

5. Share ideas with the class.

Variations

- As a class, you could develop a character who is embarking on a quest and then choose three of the hazards the children have made up and use these in a class poem, describing how the character succeeds/fails in his quest.

Cross-curricular link

- History – ideas for poems can be based on real-life events from history, where people have embarked on dangerous, sometimes fatal, journeys, e.g. Scott of the Antarctic.

Chapter 2
Poetry to perform

Introduction

Performance poetry gives children the opportunity to express feelings and emotions, and raises an awareness of the reasons why a poet has written in a particular way and how he or she is trying to make the reader feel. The performer needs to consider the meaning of the words in the poem; the necessary expression and the tone used at different times; the impact on the listener; the importance of clear articulation; and the appropriate volume and pitch to be used.

There is a role for all children within a class, even if they are not natural performers. In the preparing of a poem to perform, pupils will need to plan the performance, write a script, direct the rehearsals, make any necessary props and scenery, and decide who is most suitable for each role. As the poem is performed, some pupils can be responsible for recording the performance using sound and visual equipment, taking on roles of their own. In this way everybody can be included. It is useful to select poems that have a refrain or repetition of some kind; a 'chorus' of children can then perform these parts of the poem, while the more confident performers can take on individual roles.

It is vital that children hear other people reading poems besides their class teacher and their peers. Children are extremely tolerant, but they must, at times, become a little tired of hearing our voice day in day out. The ideal is to invite a poet to come to school and read and perform their poems. However, this is not likely to be a regular occurrence (due to financial restrictions), and so the next best thing is to find recordings of poems being read and performed. There are plenty of examples online; in the introduction to this book I have included advice on how to download from YouTube, which has a wealth of resources.

This chapter has five activities suitable for both KS1 and KS2, five aimed specifically at KS1 and five at KS2. However, this is only a guide and you may well find you can adapt any or all of them for your class.

A Brian Moses experience

This activity centres on the poem 'Walking with my Iguana' by Brian Moses, which can be found online at the poetry archive. This is an excellent website with recordings of poets reading their own poems.

Suitable for

KS1
KS2

Aims

- To recognise the strategies used when performing a poem.
- To perform a poem, focusing on expression, tone, volume and articulation.

Resources

- 'Walking With My Iguana' by Brian Moses: www.poetryarchive.org/childrensarchive/singlePoem.do?poemId=52
- Percussion instruments (optional)

What to do

1. Look up Brian Moses on the website and find out some facts about him. It is always good to do this before exploring poets' work, as it provides pupils with a useful background context.
2. Play the poem. Children find the poem and the way it is read very amusing and will undoubtedly want it played again! It is important to do this before entering into discussion, so that pupils can absorb the rhythms and patterns of the performance.
3. Ask pupils to identify the strategies used to make this an effective performance, e.g. use of tone and expression, funny voices and musical accompaniment.

> 4. In groups, ask the children to discuss how they would like to perform this poem. Give them the opportunity to use either body percussion or actual percussion instruments. Possibly divide the poem up and allot each group a section to prepare and then put the poem together and perform. Alternatively, ask each group to prepare the whole poem and then compare performances. This would be a good opportunity for self- and peer assessment.

Variations

- With younger children, rather than putting together their own performance, they could play along with the Brian Moses version, joining in with key words and phrases and putting their own percussion to the original.

Cross-curricular links

- Music – focusing on rhythm, volume and pitch.
- ICT – record the performances and use the playback to make any necessary improvements.

Water, water, everywhere

The poem used in this activity gives children the opportunity to explore the many sounds made by water. When performing the poem they can think of different ways by which to represent these sounds.

Suitable for

KS1
KS2

Aims

- To identify effective ways of performing poems.

Resources

- 'Water' by Andrew Collett: http://wackyverse.free-hostin.com/main.htm

What to do

1. Ask the children to think about water and the many different places where water can be found. Make a list on the board, e.g. the sea, tap water, rain, lakes etc. Encourage the children to think about the different sounds water can make, depending on where it is situated. Record the different sounds they think of on the board.
2. Read 'Water' by Andrew Collett, asking the children to identify the sources of water that the poet identifies. Reread the poem and have a copy on the board for the children to see. As you read, highlight any verbs or adjectives that give information about water, e.g. 'rivers rush' and 'saucepans sizzle'.
3. Divide the class into four groups and explain that each group is going to perform one verse, thinking of the most effective ways to represent the different sounds water makes. If you have

percussion instruments then the children could use these, or else encourage them to use objects around the room or body percussion.
4. Perform the poem, with each group presenting their verse.

Variations

* This poem contains many onomatopoeic words and this could be the focus for the performance, with children finding ways to represent words such as 'crash' and 'sizzle'. They could also begin to create a word bank of onomatopoeias to use later in their own poems.

Cross-curricular links

Music – this is the obvious link, encouraging children to explore, choose and organise sounds.

Science – a common topic in science is the water cycle, and this would be a fun poem to use during this unit of work.

Performing as teachers

Poems that describe people are very useful for turning into a performance. The poem used in this activity is all about teachers, so the children should love acting this out!

Suitable for

KS1
KS2

Aims

- To use language and actions to explore and convey characteristics.

Resources

- 'Teachers' by Roger Stevens: www.shavick.com/guestpoet.htm

What to do

1. Read the poem 'Teachers' by Roger Stevens. You might like, at this point, to also explore the website above, where there is an interview with Roger. In the interview he discusses his writing and then dedicates the poems on the page to all school children.
2. Divide the class into five groups and allot each group eight lines to learn and to prepare a performance linked with these lines. Explain to the children that they do not have to just read the lines out continuously; they might want to act out little scenes after a few words or a couple of lines. For example, where the poem talks about teachers having eyes in the back of their head, the group could act a short classroom scene, where the teacher calls out warnings to the children, even though her back is turned. Emphasise the idea that they should try to portray the particular characteristics of teachers as clearly as possible.

> 3. In this way, the children will be creating five scenes that depict the ideas in the poem. When they have had plenty of time to practise, put the whole poem together (preferably using a large space like the hall or stage).

Variations

- With older children, each group might want to perform the whole poem, and then it would be interesting to evaluate how each group decides to represent the ideas.

Cross-curricular links

Literacy – biographies and autobiographies. Children could explore the poet, using the interview on the website as a starting point.

Acting up

This activity will really encourage children to use their acting skills, performing a poem as if it were a miniature play. Great fun!

Suitable for

KS1
KS2

Aims

- To create, adapt and sustain different roles, individually and in groups.

Resources

- 'Adventures of Isabel' by Ogden Nash: www.poemhunter.com/poem/adventures-of-isabel/

What to do

1. Explain to the children that they are going to change a poem into a four-act play. The poem has four stanzas and is full of action and excitement so should make an excellent performance.
2. Read 'Adventures of Isabel' by Ogden Nash. Discuss the four stanzas. Reread the poem and then ask the children to retell it as a story (this will familiarise them with the key incidents and the vocabulary).
3. Divide the children into groups and ask each group to choose a stanza that they would like to change into a scene for a play (if there are arguments, you will have to draw lots). Explain that they can use the words from the poem if they wish, or they can make up their own dialogue – it is up to them – but the main theme of each stanza should remain the same.
4. Give the children time to prepare and practise their scene and then use a large space – preferably the hall or a stage – to perform the poem as a play.

Variations

- This poem could be made into a wonderful cartoon strip. The children could work in groups to represent each stanza as part of a cartoon. If you have animation software in your school, you might be able to use this.

Cross-curricular links

ICT – see ideas in Variations above.
Art – see ideas in Variations above.

Going solo

This activity needs to be used when the children are familiar and confident with performance poetry, as it requires them to work more independently.

Suitable for

KS1
KS2

Aims

- To use ICT software as part of a poetry performance.

Resources

- Access to computers and software that allows children to present a slide show with imported images and words
- A wide selection of poems

What to do

1. Explain to the children that they have now had plenty of practice with performing poems, particularly in groups or as a class. They are now going to have a go at preparing a poem by themselves, using an ICT-based presentation as part of the performance. If possible, have an example ready that you have prepared: you read a poem, and as you do so, a presentation is shown, which could include images, sound effects, words, animations etc.
2. Ask the children to take some time to choose a favourite poem. Encourage them to think about choosing a poem that will be effective when performed.
3. Give them time to work with the ICT software, designing a presentation to go with their poem. It would be better if they were

familiar with the software from previous ICT sessions, but if not, you could spend some time demonstrating the key tools they might use. With younger children, it might be useful to prepare a presentation altogether before they attempt to do this alone.

4. Each day, at the beginning and end of the day, you could share a presentation or two and then discuss whether the ICT part of the performance enhances or detracts from the effectiveness of the poem.

Variations

- This activity does not have to be based on ICT. The children could use props and masks and costumes as part of their performance.

Cross-curricular links

ICT – the obvious link!
DT – designing and making props and masks for the performances.

Have fun joining in

This is a simple introduction to performance poetry for younger children. They can feel involved and have fun without any particular pressure.

Suitable for

KS1

Aims

- To understand that poems can be performed.

Resources

- 'The Cupboard' by Walter de la Mare (Appendix 1d)
- If possible:
    - A small key
    - Some cakes
    - A jar of lollipops

What to do

1. Read the poem 'The Cupboard' by Walter de la Mare, using the props as you go along.
2. Reread the poem. What do you notice about it? Identify the repetition of 'me, me, me' in stanzas one, two and four and the slight change in stanza three where the words are 'with the key, key, key'.
3. Explain to the children that they are going to help you to perform the poem. Ask a volunteer to hold the key, another to hold the cakes and another to hold the jar of lollipops. They need to think of an action they will do with their prop when it comes to that part of the poem. The rest of the class will also have a task: when it comes to the final line of each stanza, they have to join in (remembering the slight change in stanza three).

> 4. Reread the poem, with the children joining in. Explain that you are all performing, rather than just reciting, the poem. Have another go and then if you have the time and opportunity, perform to another class in the school.

Variations

- Children could use percussion instruments to emphasise the final lines of each stanza, marking the beat of the words 'me, me, me' and 'key, key, key'.

Cross·curricular links

Spelling – noticing that words that sound the same can sometimes be spelt differently, e.g. 'key' and 'me' and 'knee'.

Sing along with the chicken song

This activity is all about giving young children the opportunity to join in with poems and to make them their own through performance and music.

Suitable for

KS1

Aims

- To promote the links between music and performance poetry.

Resources

- 'The Egg Song' by Tony Mitton: http://heatheranne.freeservers.com/childrens/TheEggSong.htm

What to do

1. Read 'The Egg Song' by Tony Mitton, with the poem displayed on the board. What do the children like about the poem? What are their favourite words/lines?
2. Reread the poem, encouraging the children to join in where they wish to. Talk about the words used and the rhythm and rhyme and how they might want to make up a tune for the chick's song.
3. Discuss ways of performing the poem. Children could split into groups and one group could be the narrators for the first two verses, while another group provides an accompaniment of 'pecking' noises using percussion instruments. There could be a group who are going to act and sing as the chick and they will need support with creating a tune and working out actions that they might use as part of their performance.
4. Alternatively, the whole class could work together, all helping to create a tune and all performing the poem together.
5. The poem could be performed to another class/parents/in an assembly.

Variations

- This would be a good opportunity to explore the way that music represents certain feelings and concepts. What instruments do the children choose to represent the sound of the chick pecking? Discussion could take place about other animals and what sounds would best represent them, e.g. elephant and drum.

Cross-curricular links

Music – how music can be used to portray different concepts.
Science – lifecycles.

Performing favourite poems

It is important that children begin to develop favourite poems from a young age. One of the best ways to begin this is to listen to the poet reciting his or her poem and then learn it 'off by heart' and produce a performance.

Suitable for

KS1

Aims

- To help children to identify favourite poems and learn them 'off by heart'.

Resources

- Poems by Allan Ahlberg: a selection can be found at www.poetryarchive.org/childrensarchive/singlePoet.do?poetId=81
- You do not have to use Ahlberg, but this poet has written poems that both children and adults often identify as favourites, so you are probably on to a winner if you choose him

What to do

1. Play a selection of Ahlberg's poems, which can be found at the website above. Discuss which are the children's favourites and why this is.
2. Explain to the children that, as a class, they are going to learn the poem 'Billy McBone' and perform it. Replay the poem and discuss the repetition of the lines 'Billy McBone/Had a mind of his own' and ask the class to repeat these lines so that they can remember them by heart.
3. Discuss the fact that the third and sixth lines rhyme, which makes it easy to predict what the final word of line six might be. Look carefully at the different rhymes – 'hat' and 'that', 'ears' and 'years', 'saw' and 'floor', 'key' and 'free'. Say one of these words to the children,

> e.g. 'hat', and see if they can remember the word that rhymes with hat. The fourth and fifth lines also rhyme and these could be explored in the same way.
>
> 4. Ask the children to identify the short piece of dialogue in the poem – where the teacher speaks – and perform this yourself in a very 'teacherly' voice.
> 5. Replay the whole poem, asking the children to join in whenever they remember a word or a rhyme. Remind the children of the first two lines of each verse and say that you are going to recite the poem, but they are going to do these first two lines. Count them in and off you go! This performance can be improved/altered with each practice, until the children are eventually reciting the whole poem without support.

Variations

- Encourage the children to bring in favourite poems/rhymes/songs from home and support them with teaching these favourites to the rest of the class.

Cross-curricular links

Music – encourage the children to sing favourite songs and rhymes, identifying why they have these as favourites.

A journey through the year

This activity requires the children to make props before they even hear the poem. They can then use what they have made as part of the performance.

Suitable for

KS1

Aims

- To use a performance poem to help with learning the months of the year.

Resources

- 'The Garden Year' by Sara Coleridge: www.poets.org/viewmedia.php/prmMID/20287
- A4 paper and art materials

What to do

1. Ask the children if they know the months of the year. Recite altogether the months and group them under the four seasons.
2. Discuss characteristics of particular months, e.g. February might be freezing cold and snowy; December brings Christmas; September is back to school time.
3. Ask the children to choose a month and to draw/paint a picture to show some aspect of that month. Suggest that they might want to use colours that are associated with particular months, e.g. yellow with August, green with the spring months.
4. When the children have completed their pictures, read them the poem 'The Garden Year' by Sara Coleridge. Explain that you are going to work together to produce a class performance of the poem, with the children standing up and saying their month at the beginning

of each stanza and holding up their picture. You will read the remaining words in each stanza. Model this, so that everyone knows what is expected.

5. Perform the poem and discuss the performance. Have another go and make any improvements. Ask a volunteer to recite the months of the year.

Variations

- If the children feel confident, they could learn the whole verse that relates to their picture and recite it as they hold up their art work.

Cross-curricular link

Art – the obvious link! Using colours and shades to represent concepts.

Playing schools

> With this activity, children can just enjoy acting and performing. There is no pressure to remember words or recite lines, so all pupils should be able to join in.

Suitable for

KS1

Aims

- To use language and actions to explore and convey situations, characters and emotions.

Resources

- 'Please Mrs Butler' by Allan Ahlberg: www.poetryarchive.org/childrensarchive/singlePoem.do?poemId=82

What to do

1. Play the poem 'Please Mrs Butler' by Allan Ahlberg. On the website above, Ahlberg is reading the poem himself. Before he reads it, he gives a little introduction about the amount of questions a teacher is asked during a day and how this was the inspiration for the poem.
2. Discuss the poem and explain to the children that they are going to get into pairs and decide on how they might act out this poem, with one child as the teacher and one child as the pupil. They do not have to include any words if they do not wish to, as they will be acting alongside the recital by Ahlberg. They will, however, need to make their actions very clear, so that an audience is able to tell who is the teacher and who is the pupil. You may wish to model this, so that the children are clear about what is expected (although there are no hard and fast rules).

> 3. Replay the poem, so that the class are really familiar with all the verses. Give children time to prepare their performance.
> 4. Play the poem and, as it is played, the children act out their performances. If there is time, some pairings may wish to show their performance to the class.

Variations

- If the children are not confident to work in pairs, you could act as the teacher and they could all be the pupils. They may then feel that they can have a go independently.

Cross-curricular links

Drama – conveying meaning through body language, facial expressions etc.

A feline mystery

This activity uses the well-known poem 'Macavity the Mystery Cat', by T S Eliot. The wonderful language and rhythm of this poem make it an excellent choice for performing. There is a useful video clip of Michael Rosen reciting the poem at the website shown below.

Suitable for

KS2

Aims

- To focus on articulation, volume and pitch.

Resources

- 'Macavity the Mystery Cat' by T S Eliot: www.love-poems.me.uk/ eliot_macavity_the_mystery_cat.htm
- 'Macavity the Mystery Cat' read by Michael Rosen: www.bbc.co.uk/schools/ teachers/offbyheart/video/michael_rosen_macavity.shtml

What to do

1. Explain to the class that they are going to hear a poem and you would like them to focus not only on the words but also on how it is read.
2. Play 'Macavity the Mystery Cat': www.bbc.co.uk/schools/teachers/ offbyheart/video/michael_rosen_macavity.shtml
3. What do you notice about the performance? Discuss as a class. What makes a good performance?
4. Give every child a copy of the words of the poem (or put an enlarged version on the board). Read through the poem, ensuring that the children understand the meaning of all the words (it is very difficult to perform a poem effectively if you are unsure of the meaning). Discuss any difficult/unusual vocabulary.

> 5. Play the poem again, asking the children to join in with key phrases. What are the important aspects of performing poetry? Discuss articulation, volume, pitch, facial expression etc.

Variations

• Children could create a class performance of this poem, perhaps using masks and other props made in art or DT. This could be performed in an assembly or end-of-year production.

Cross·curricular links

Art/DT – making props/masks to wear during performance.

All aboard

Rhythm and tempo are a vital aspect of performance poetry. This activity provides opportunities for children to explore how a poet deliberately uses particular words and line lengths in order to promote a particular rhythmic effect.

Suitable for

KS2

Aims

- To recognise how poets create particular effects.

Resources

- 'Night Train' by W H Auden: www.tynelives.org.uk/stephenson/poem.htm and www.screenonline.org.uk/film/id/530415/ – go to the video clips section on the right of the screen and choose 'Night Mail'. This link takes you to an excellent black and white video of the night train, with the poem being read in the background

What to do

1. Ask the children to think about the sounds they associate with trains. Discuss this in small groups and feed back to the whole class. Focus on the rhythmic, repetitive sound of a train passing along railway tracks.
2. Play the video clip found on the website above. This video clip is in black and white and is incredibly atmospheric. In the background, the poem by Auden is read aloud and the reader emphasises the changing rhythms – as the train picks up speed, slows down, draws into the station. You may want to play this a couple of times to allow the children to really absorb the rhythm of the poem.

3. Discuss how Auden creates this effect, using words and lines of different lengths, specific numbers of syllables in words, rhyme and making changes to the flow of the poem as the train alters its speed.
4. Divide the children into groups and give each group a particular section of the poem to prepare. Ask them to think about how they have heard the poem being read, but to consider how they might like to perform the poem – they may have other ideas. Give the groups time to prepare their section and then perform the whole poem, with each group chiming in as it gets to their part. Evaluate the performance – were there any words/lines that they found particularly effective?

Variations

- Instead of reciting the poem as part of the performance, the children could put a musical accompaniment to the poem as it is read on the film clip. This would give them the opportunity to use appropriate instruments to represent the speed and rhythm and would increase the focus on word and line structure as they match music to poem.

Cross-curricular links

Music – see Variations above.
History – focusing on railways and the evolution of train travel.

Double, double, toil and trouble

It would not be right to have a poetry book without an activity relating to William Shakespeare. I decided to choose 'The Witches' Spell' in this section as it lends itself wonderfully to performance poetry and is accessible for children.

Suitable for

KS2

Aims

● To familiarise children with the language and style of Shakespeare's poetry.

Resources

● 'The Witches' Spell' by William Shakespeare (Appendix 1e). It is also available at: http://poetry.about.com/library/weekly/blshakespearehalloween.htm

What to do

1. Provide the children with a little background information about the witches scene in Macbeth – the witches are making prophesies about how things will turn out for Macbeth. Their spell-making is always set against a background of terrible weather and storms, creating a terrifyingly evil atmosphere. The witches always speak in rhyming couplets, distinguishing them from the other characters in the play.

2. Give every child a copy of the witches scene and ask them to read it through in groups – make these groups mixed ability, so that the more confident readers can support the less confident. When they have had some time to absorb the style and language, ask if there are any volunteers who would read particular parts. Read through the poem, with different children taking on the different roles. Repeat this as many times as is necessary, so that everyone who wants to has the opportunity to read.

3. Assign each group a role – if you have six groups, have two groups for each witch. Set up the classroom with a 'cauldron' in the middle and plenty of space all around. All children to encircle the cauldron and enact the witches scene, with each group reciting their part.

4. At a later date it would be great to make props and put together costumes so that this could become a full performance.

Variations

- Children could be split into groups of three and put together their own interpretation of the scene, eventually performing to the class. This would promote the opportunity to self- and peer-evaluate and could lead to some excellent discussions about how Shakespeare uses language so effectively.

Cross-curricular links

History – Shakespeare is a key figure who is often studied when children are exploring the Elizabethan era. The use of Macbeth and this particular scene would extend children's understanding of this great man and the beliefs that were held about witches at this time in history.

Let battle commence!

This activity combines poetry, performance, music and history – what more could you ask for?

Suitable for

KS2

Aims

● To adapt speech for a range of audiences and purposes.

Resources

● 'Drake's Drum' by Sir Henry Newbolt (Appendix 1f)
● www.olimu.com/readings/DrakesDrum.htm
● Drums

What to do

1. Access the website above. This gives some background information upon which the poem is based. This is useful contextualisation and encourages children to think about how legends and poems 'grow' from real life, historic events.
2. If you scroll down the web page, you will find a link that has a reading of the poem. It is well read and you can sit back, relax and enjoy the recital!
3. Discuss the idea of performing this poem. What ideas do the children have? How might you use drums as an accompaniment to a performance? Give the children time to come up with some ideas and then share with the class.
4. Ask the children to decide whether they would like to produce a class performance, with everyone involved (individuals reciting, groups joining in with the 'Capten, art tha sleepin' there below?' line,

drummers etc.) or if they would like to work in groups to produce different performances.
5. Give children time to prepare their performance (you may need ear plugs!). This would make a great idea for a class assembly, with some children introducing the topic and discussing Sir Francis Drake, what the drum was used for, where the drum is kept now etc. and then performing the poem.

Variations

- If you do not have a great deal of time, the children could work out a drumming pattern and they could play this alongside the reading on the web page above.

Cross-curricular links

History – sixteenth-century explorers.
Music – composing accompaniments to poems.

For whom the bell tolls

Like the previous activity, this is based on a seafaring poem. It is a great tale and has a good moral, as well as making a fantastic poem to perform.

Suitable for

KS2

Aims

- To evaluate how they and others have contributed to the overall effectiveness of performances.

Resources

- 'Ballad of Inchcape Rock' by Robert Southey (see Appendix 1g)
- www.mainlesson.com/display.php?author=burt&book=poems&story= inchcape
- Some useful notes about the poem: http://wiki.answers.com/Q/ What_is_the_Summary_of_the_poem_Inchcape_Rock&src=ansTT

What to do

1. If you access the first website above, there is a copy of the poem 'Ballad of Inchcape Rock' by Robert Southey; it should be in large enough font for the class to be able to see. Introduce the poem by giving a summary of the plot (see the second website above) and then ask if there are any volunteers who would like to read a verse.
2. Read the poem, with children doing a verse each. Discuss the ideas in the poem – the moral, how the person who committed the evil deed got his comeuppance – and the structure of the poem – its rhyme and rhythm and regular stanzas.

3. Discuss how this poem might be performed and encourage the children to work together to plan and prepare a performance. Explain that the performance will be recorded and then they will watch it played back and evaluate their own performances. Give them time to prepare.

4. Perform the poem and record the performance. Encourage children to evaluate their own and others' performances. What was really good about it? What might be improved? If there is time, the children could make the necessary changes, perform again and re-evaluate.

Variations

● This poem would have fitted just as well into the narrative poetry chapter. The children could either write and perform a play script based on the poem, or practise retelling the poem in narrative form.

Cross-curricular links

Geography – Inchcape Rock or the Bell Rock is a real-life reef in Scotland, with a lighthouse called the Bell Rock Lighthouse. Children could use Google Earth to explore the location and the geological features.

Chapter 3
Humorous poetry and word play

Introduction

One of the joys of teaching poetry is being able to make children laugh, tapping into their sense of humour and creating an environment where laughter and an understanding of how language can amuse and entertain is shared and appreciated. There are many poems, anthologies of poems and websites dedicated to humorous verse, and these are excellent starting points to capture the interest of young learners and motivate them to explore the potential of language.

Playing with words, manipulating language for your own use and understanding 'hidden' meanings in texts where the author or poet has exploited language for a particular purpose are all essential life skills. By engaging with poems that play with language, children are not just 'doing literacy' – they are adding to their knowledge and understanding of the world and are developing an insight into how oral and written language has both a purpose and an audience that need to be considered and accounted for.

Most children are familiar with a range of nursery rhymes, tongue twisters, riddles and nonsense verse. They are also usually aware that there are alternative versions that can be read and quoted (not always appropriate unfortunately!). The alternative versions are often amusing and rely on a knowledge and understanding of the original concept and vocabulary. They usually follow a similar structure, rhythm and rhyme to the original and therefore provide a useful structure for children to utilise for their own poetry writing.

In this chapter I have tried to draw on all these aspects of humorous verse and word play and have included nine activities that are suitable for both KS1 and KS2 and three activities specific to KS1 and three to KS2. With this theme, however, most children will enjoy all the activities as they allow them to indulge in the lighter side of life, so have a good look through and enjoy them all!

Teachers under the weather

Children love to be able to make fun of their teachers. This activity allows them to do this (in a gentle way!) by comparing teachers to different types of weather.

Suitable for

KS1
KS2

Aims

- To recognise how humour can be created by linking two unrelated concepts, i.e. teachers and weather.

Resources

- 'Good Morning this is the Teacher Forecast' by David Calder: www .windowsproject.demon.co.uk/publish/davecalder/youngread/poems3.htm
- Examples of weather forecasts: http://news.bbc.co.uk/weather/

What to do

1. Ask the children the question, 'If you were a type of weather, what would you be?' Give an example, e.g. someone with a fierce temper might be a hurricane – loud and dangerous. Allow the children some time to discuss this in pairs.
2. Read an example of a weather forecast, using the BBC website as shown above. Discuss with the children the way these tend to be written/read out and ask some volunteers to read out a forecast in the style of a weather forecaster from the television.
3. Read the poem 'Good Morning this is the Teacher Forecast' by David Calder. This poem is in the style of a weather report, attaching

particular weathers to certain teachers. Ask a volunteer to read the poem in the style of a weather reporter. Discuss how the poet has created his humorous effects, by describing the teachers in terms of their similarity to types of weather. The humour results directly from the clever imitation of a real weather forecast, with the specific use of metaphor (KS2 children could focus on this particular linguistic device).

4. Children could then choose teachers they know and describe them in terms of particular weather conditions (with the warning that they need to be polite!). If each group chose a different teacher, ultimately all the groups' ideas could be put together to make a class poem.

Variations

- If a class poem has been written, children could present this in the style of a weather report, and others could record it. This could then be played back, edited and rerecorded, to produce a polished final performance, suitable for an outside audience.

Cross-curricular link

ICT – the use of recording devices and then moving on to the editing and rerecording, aiming to produce a good-quality final product.

Science – types of weather and the scientific vocabulary used to describe them.

Nursery rhyme bonanza

This activity is a useful way to engage all children (especially reluctant readers/writers) through using the familiarity of an age-old poetic form.

Suitable for

KS1
KS2

Aims

- To use the structure and familiarity of nursery rhymes as scaffolds for poetry writing.

Resources

- Access to a range of nursery rhymes – originals and alternative versions
- 'Humpty's Big Fall' by Kenn Nesbitt: www.poetry4kids.com/poem-535.html
- 'Hickory, Dickory, Dock' by Kenn Nesbitt: www.poetry4kids.com/poem-537 .html

What to do

1. Choose two or three popular nursery rhymes and ask children to recite them from memory (it may be that they use different versions at this stage and this can be discussed – the oral tradition of nursery rhymes means that there are often variations in the language).
2. Read them some alternative versions – Kenn Nesbitt's 'Humpty's Big Fall' and 'Hickory, Dickory, Dock'.
3. Have an original and an alternative written out on the board. Ask children to point out where and how they differ.
4. Shared writing – ask children to choose an original nursery rhyme. As a class, choose which parts will change and which will stay

> the same. Gradually build up a class version on board, with teacher as scribe. KS2 children could then make up their own verses and these could all be put together as a class book of alternative rhymes.

Variations

- This activity can be used to promote children's ability to recognise spelling patterns in words. Nursery rhymes generally rhyme, and analogies can be drawn between different words, e.g. fall, wall, call. If alternative versions are being created within the class, banks of words could first be collected that all have the same spelling pattern. This might also be a good time to identify words that sound the same but are spelt differently, e.g. light, kite, white. Julia Donaldson's picture books (often written in rhyme) are very useful for this type of activity.

Cross-curricular links

History – it would be interesting for children to research the origins of certain nursery rhymes so that they are aware of when and why they were written. By creating their own nursery rhymes, they themselves become part of history.

What nonsense!

Spike Milligan is a real favourite with many children. His wacky and wonderful verses delight and entertain. This activity allows children the freedom to be wacky too!

Suitable for

KS1
KS2

Aims

- To recognise how poets use nonsense words to create wacky poems.

Resources

- 'The Land of the Bumbly Boo' by Spike Milligan: www.poetryarchive.org/childrensarchive/singlePoem.do?poemId=7514
- 'On the Ning Nang Nong' by Spike Milligan: www.poetryarchive.org/childrensarchive/singlePoem.do?poemId=7515

What to do

1. Ask the children what they think 'nonsense' means. Discuss the word and ask if they ever speak nonsense or are told they are speaking nonsense. Explain that speaking nonsense can be very useful, especially with poetry.
2. Play the poem 'The Land of the Bumbly Boo' (using the website above, the children can listen to Spike reciting the poem). Give children copies of the poem and allow them time in their groups to discuss the language used and how the poet creates the desired effect. What images are created in your mind? Ask volunteers to read the poem aloud, with the whole class joining in with key words and phrases.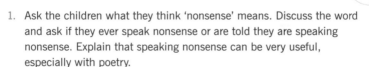

3. Repeat with 'On the Ning Nang Nong' – again by Spike Milligan (this poem is also available on the website).

4. Ask the children to choose one of the words from the poems, e.g. 'clang' or 'ping' or 'bumbly', and to build up a list of nonsense words that rhyme with the chosen word. Using Milligan's versions, they can then replace his words with their own nonsense words to create a nonsense poem of their own.

Variations

• These poems could be used to introduce the idea of onomatopoeia and how this linguistic device can be used to create particular effects when writing poems or stories. Children could develop lists of onomatopoeias, connected with different topics, e.g. the topic of water could inspire words such as 'splash' and 'whoosh' and keep these in their writing journals for use at a later date.

Cross-curricular links

Art – the images created by Spike Milligan in his poetry could be used as inspirations for children's artwork. This would make a wonderful display, with red, white and blue people, foxes in pink boxes, and cats wearing trousers and hats!

Tongue twister torture

When children are given the opportunity to play with words, it helps them to remember them – how to read them and how to spell them. This tongue twister activity will have them in stitches!

Suitable for

KS1
KS2

Aims

- To raise awareness of the sounds that words make.

Resources

- A range of tongue twisters. Here are some examples:
- 'The Cow' by Jack Prelutsky: www.mrsduvallsclass.com/Moo.htm
- Animated tongue twisters: www.indianchild.com/animated_tongue_twisters .htm
- More tricky tongue twisters: www.fun-with-words.com/tong_example.html

What to do

1. Ask the children if they know of any tongue twisters and ask them to recite them to the class. If they are confident they could teach the class their tongue twister.
2. Share some different tongue twisters and encourage children to practise reciting them (this will cause much amusement!).
3. Read 'The Cow' by Jack Prelutsky, making sure that the children can all see a copy of the poem as you read it. What is the dominant sound in the word? It is the 'oo' sound. How many different ways

are there of spelling the 'oo' sound in this poem? – 'oo', 'ew', 'u-e'. Some words rhyme and yet are spelt differently.

4. Go back to some of the tongue twisters you looked at earlier. Can you find any other examples where words sound the same but are spelt differently?

Variations

- Tongue twisters can be used to improve children's pronunciation and enunciation. You could choose a tongue twister, and have a fun competition to see who can make the fewest mistakes in reciting it.

Cross-curricular links

Literacy – this activity raises an awareness of how words sound and how they are spelt. You could extend this into regular spelling sessions where, instead of merely learning lists of words, children could undertake their own research and find poems that use particular spelling patterns. Julia Donaldson's picture books, in rhyme, would be useful for this.

It's riddle time!

Riddles are a great way to encourage children to use language effectively. In this activity, children need to look closely at the vocabulary used in the riddles, in order to make an informed guess as to what the riddle is referring to.

Suitable for

KS1
KS2

Aims

- To recognise the power of language, when it is used effectively.

Resources

- A range of riddles. Here are some examples:
- 'Bluebottle' by Judith Nicholls: www.poetryarchive.org/childrensarchive/ singlePoem.do?poemId=400
- A great website with many riddles is: www.landofmagic.co.uk/ riddles_to_solve.htm

What to do

1. What is a riddle? What is the intention of the writer when they create a riddle? To give useful clues, without giving away the answer.
2. Read a selection of riddles and encourage the children to work in pairs to find the answers. Begin with some easy riddles where the writer gives plenty of transparent clues. Ask the children how they have reached their answer – what were the key words that helped them?

3. Give the children some more riddles that are a little more difficult to solve. Why are these more difficult? Explore the language that the writer has used.
4. Ask the children to choose their favourite riddle and pay a visit to another class where the children can test out their riddles on others.

Variations

* Once the children have had the opportunity to read and share plenty of riddles, they will probably want to make up their own. This would be a useful task for homework or during free writing time. These riddles could be made into a class book. Alternatively, you could have a 'riddle box' in the classroom; when children have made up a riddle, they could post it into the box at the end of the week, the box could be opened and the riddles shared with the class.

Cross-curricular links

Science – creating riddles linked to science topics would be a good way of familiarising children with the subject-specific vocabulary. For example, when learning about forces, children could write a riddle about the wind or magnets, choosing relevant vocabulary to provide the clues.

Alphabetic animals

Alphabet poems are always popular. Edward Lear's poem 'An Animal Alphabet' is complete nonsense and great fun. This activity gives children the freedom to be as crazy with words as they like!

Suitable for

KS1
KS2

Aims

- To give children the opportunity to play with words.

Resources

- 'An Animal Alphabet' by Edward Lear: www.nonsenselit.org/Lear/MN/nr1.html
- A3 paper

What to do

1. Give each child in the class a piece of A3 paper with a letter of the alphabet printed on it. Explain that you are going to read them an alphabet poem and as they hear the verse that relates to their letter, they need to stand and hold up their piece of paper.
2. Read 'An Animal Alphabet' by Edward Lear. Give the children time to discuss and to explore the very strange vocabulary. Talk about the use of alliteration and how this emphasises each letter of the alphabet.
3. Give each child/pair of children the verse that corresponds with their letter and give them some time to practise reading the words and (if they wish to) learning them. With KS1, put the children in

mixed ability pairs so that they can support each other with the reading, and just give them the first line of each verse to learn (the alliteration should make these lines easy to recite). With KS2 children, one child in the pair could recite the first line – which introduces the animal – and the other child could learn lines two and three – which always begin with 'who ....'

4. Reread the whole poem to the class, so that you are modelling the correct pronunciation of the difficult vocabulary. Collect in the A3 paper with the alphabet letters and reverse roles so that the children are reciting their verses while you are holding up the letters.

Variations

- This would be a great starting point for some poetry writing. Using the alphabet as the basis for their poems, the children could each choose a letter, then find an animal and choose some exciting adjectives to describe the animal, and then make up two crazy lines to describe an action/activity relating to their animal. The verses could then be put together to make a class poem.

Cross-curricular links

Art – it would be wonderful to illustrate this crazy poem. Although this would be suitable for both key stages, it might be more appropriate for KS1 to produce illustrations for the poem, if they found it difficult to read the original. They could then hold up their pictures as the poem was read aloud.

Metaphor madness

This activity introduces how metaphor can be used to play with words. This may seem a difficult concept for younger children, but you do not necessarily have to go into technical detail – just enjoy the poem!

Suitable for

KS1
KS2

Aims

* To recognise how poets use words for particular effects.

Resources

* 'Poetry Pie' by Tony Mitton: www.tonymitton.co.uk/#/poetry-pie/
  4534268915

What to do

1. What do you think a poetry pie would look like? What might you put in a poetry pie? Words? Ideas? Feelings? Give the children the opportunity to discuss this concept. Can we really have a poetry pie?
2. Read 'Poetry Pie' by Tony Mitton. Using a pie as a metaphor, Mitton manages to make the idea of poetry mouth-watering. Look carefully at how he links references to actual pies, e.g. 'meaty' and 'fruity' with poetry references, e.g. 'rhythm' and 'rhyme'.
3. In the last line, the poet invites us to taste a piece of poetry pie. How might we do this? What does he mean? We could taste poetry by exploring lots of poems and finding which ones we like best – just as we do with different foods.

4. Invite the children to create a recipe for poetry pizza. What might you include on a poetry pizza? Anchovies and adjectives, slices of rhyme, words that melt in your mouth like the cheesy topping? Give the children time to come up with some ideas for their poetry pizza and then share with the class.

Variations

- The children could write a set of instructions, e.g. how to make a poetry pie: first create a pie case of ideas; next collect your word ingredients to include adjectives, similes, metaphors etc.

Cross-curricular links

Music – I think the poem 'Poetry Pie' would be wonderful set to music. It has a strong rhythm that lends itself to being sung. The children could work together to put this poem to music.

Silent letters

Silent letters in words can often cause children great problems when reading and spelling. This activity raises their awareness of silent letters, and they can have great fun making up new words of their own.

Suitable for

KS1
KS2

Aims

- To recognise silent letters in words.

Resources

- 'Pterence Pterodactyl' by Ptrevor Millum: www.trevormillum.co.uk/ poems_stories/poetry_gallery/poem5.htm
- www.bbc.co.uk/skillswise/words/spelling/soundandspell/silentletters/flash0. shtml – this website has an interactive game to reinforce children's understanding of silent letters

What to do

1. What words do you know that have silent letters? Write any examples on the board. If the children are not sure, give them some examples, e.g. 'knight', 'know', 'pneumonia' and 'psychic'.
2. Have the poem 'Pterence Pterodactyl' by Ptrevor Millum on the board so that the children are able to see it as well as hear you read it. Read the poem as if you are supposed to pronounce the 'p' at the beginning of each word. Ask the children what was wrong with this reading. Reread (or ask a volunteer to read the poem) correctly, not pronouncing the 'p' at the beginning of each word.

3. Have the children noticed that the poet has only put a 'p' at the beginning of the words that begin with a 't'? Why has he done this?
4. Go to the BBC website shown above. On this site there is a 'Save the World' game that children can play, based on recognition of silent letters. There are different levels and speeds, so you can choose to suit the age and ability of your children. Demonstrate the game to the class and then you could either take turns and play as a class on the board or, if you have access to a computer suite, children could play independently.
5. Once the children have had time to play the game, share any new words they have learnt that have silent letters. These could be displayed as a word bank to support children with their spelling.

Variations

● The poem 'Pterence Pterodactyl' could be used as a model for children's own poems where they play with silent letters to create new words.

Cross-curricular links

Spelling – this activity will raise children's awareness of the cruel nature of English spelling!

Hunting for homophones

Children can have great fun with homophones. Once they start to find them, you won't be able to stop them hunting for more!

Suitable for

KS1
KS2

Aims

- To identify and recognise homophones.

Resources

- Examples of poems using homophones:
  - http://j.whyville.net/smmk/whytimes/ article?id=3523
  - www.bbc.co.uk/skillswise/words/spelling/recognising/homophones/tutor.
    shtml
  - Homophone game: www.bbc.co.uk/skillswise/words/spelling/recognising/
    homophones/quiz.shtml

What to do

1. What is a homophone? Give the children some examples, supported with visual clues (preferably pictures and the words written out), e.g. 'pair' and 'pear', 'bear' and 'bare', 'would' and 'wood'.
2. How do we know which spelling to use? It is important to look at the context to which the word belongs and then you have to learn that if you are talking, for example, about a 'big brown bear who lives in the woods', then the spelling is different from a 'big bare bottom'!
3. Read them some examples of poems that contain homophones. Ask volunteers to come up to the board and highlight the homophones.

4. Using the website above, play the homophone game with the children (you can choose levels of difficulty). As you play the game, make a list of all the homophones that are mentioned.
5. Ask the children to begin collecting examples of homophones. They can continue this for homework or during ICT sessions when they have access to computers. These homophones could later be used to create their own poems.

Variations

- The children could create homophone dictionaries that have the words and related pictures to support understanding.

Cross-curricular links

Spelling – raising awareness of how words may sound the same but have different meanings and be spelt differently.

Animal antics

> You can never have too many animal poems! Children love to think of animals doing out-of-the-ordinary things, and they can let their own imaginations run wild.

Suitable for

KS1

Aims

- To take different views into account.

Resources

- 'I have a Hippopotamus' by Dave Calder: http://heatheranne.freeservers.com/childrens/IHaveaHippopotamus.htm

What to do

1. If you could have any animal as a pet, what animal would you choose? Give the children time to discuss this in pairs. Feed back to the whole class and encourage the children to verbalise why they would choose a particular animal. In this way, children are learning to take into account others' views and opinions.
2. What would happen if you wanted to give your new pet a bath? Would they fit? Would they make a mess? Has anyone tried bathing their dog? What is the dog's reaction?
3. Read 'I have a Hippopotamus' by Dave Calder. What would it be like to have a hippo in your house? What would your mum say?
4. Explain to the class that they are going to work in pairs to make up a short role play between two characters – a mum and a child. The child has brought an unusual pet home (they can choose which animal this might be) and they are trying to explain to their mum

why they should be allowed to keep this pet (they need to come up with some good arguments). Mum is not happy!

5. Give the children time to work on their role play and, if there is time, show some examples to the class.

Variations

- This poem could be used as a model for children's own poems, where they insert an animal of their choice instead of the word 'hippopotamus' and add details of their own where they wish to.

In opposition

Children can have great fun with this activity, whilst becoming familiar with words and their opposites.

Suitable for

KS1

Aims

● To extend their knowledge and understanding of words and their opposites.

Resources

● Dictionaries of antonyms and synonyms.

What to do

1. Ask the children to think of words to describe a tortoise, e.g. slow, lazy, determined (they are often determined to escape!). Now imagine that this is a very different tortoise – in fact, he is the complete opposite from a normal tortoise – how would you describe him now?
2. Explain to the class that you are going to write a poem altogether about animals who behave very differently from normal, so they need to think about using opposite words. Give them a few lines to show them what you mean, e.g.

    Speedy tortoise, whizzing through the grass
    Slow, lazy cheetah strolling across the plains
    Short, chubby giraffe having a nap

3. Give them some time to discuss in groups and to come up with some animals that are going to be described in exactly the opposite way to normal.
4. Continue the poem, using their ideas. If the children are confident, they could write their own poems and then share them with the class.

Variations

- This activity does not have to be based on animals. You could pick a different theme, e.g. classroom objects; the children could begin by describing various objects as they are, and then find the opposites to the adjectives they have chosen, e.g. 'hard, wooden desk' becomes 'soft, spongy desk'.

Cross-curricular links

Science – in science, children often have to be able to identify the properties of different materials, and often these properties include reference to words and their opposites, e.g. 'transparent glass' and 'opaque wood'. Links could be made between the science topic and the children's poems.

Strange homes

Silly poems are very important – they make children laugh and they create an interest in poetry so that they are keen to read and share and write their own. This activity is based on a very silly poem.

Suitable for

KS1

Aims

- To make links with existing knowledge.

Resources

- 'There Was an Old Woman' by Kenn Nesbitt: www.poetry4kids.com/poem-538.html
- The original version and another version of this poem: www.alphabet-soup.net/goose/oldwoman.html

What to do

1. Who knows the rhyme 'There Was an Old Woman Who Lived in a Shoe'? See if any of the children can recite the rhyme. Read the original version and then a 'nice' version, which can be found on the second website above. Which one do you prefer?
2. Read Kenn Nesbitt's silly version. Now which one do you prefer? What would it be like to live in a shoe?
3. If you had to live somewhere other than a house/flat/bungalow, where would you choose to live? How about in a tree house? Or a tent? Or in a burrow under the ground like a rabbit?

4. Give the children time to discuss this in pairs and then feed back to the class. Encourage the children to verbalise *why* they would choose to live in a certain place. If you have time, the children could draw their alternative homes and these could form part of a display with the three versions of 'There was an old woman'.

Variations

- You could change the theme of this activity. Rather than strange homes, you could have strange people or strange animals. There are plenty of funny poems about strange things, and these make good starting points for children's own poetry writing.

Cross-curricular links

Geography – the children could investigate different places or geographical features around the world. These would make great starting points for writing.

Playing with words

> This particular activity is based around word play and requires a real exploration of the meaning of words and phrases.

Suitable for

KS2

Aims

- To recognise how words can be 'played' with.
- To identify words and phrases that have more than one meaning.

Resources

- *Who's Been Sleeping in my Porridge* – a collection of poems by Colin McNaughton

What to do

1. Introduce the poet by using the quote mentioned above.
2. Have the poem 'Dead Funny' on the board for all to see. Ask a volunteer to read the poem. Children discuss in groups what they think about the poem and then share ideas with the class. Discuss the title – why is it called 'Dead Funny'? How is this a play on words? Do we use similar phrases in other areas of our lives (dead tired, dead to the world)? The main play on words, other than the title, is the last line, 'Rust in peace'. Discuss this.
3. Give out copies of three other poems from the anthology – 'Dead Certainty', 'Tall Story' and 'Bomb Appetit'. Ask the children to discuss these poems in their groups, explaining that the poet is playing with words in each of the poems and they have to be 'poem detectives' to try to find the hidden meanings.

4. Share ideas and record on a 'word wall' any ideas that the children come up with (this can be an ongoing wall, where children can add any examples of word play that they spot in or out of school).

Variations

- Ask the children to look carefully at television and magazine advertisements, shop names, posters etc. that use word play, and bring any findings into school to add to the word wall. These could be used later to create their own poems based on word play.

More nonsense

No book on poetry would be complete without the poem 'Jabberwocky' by Lewis Carroll. Here the children have the opportunity to explore nonsense poetry through drama.

Suitable for

KS2

Aims

- To explore nonsense poetry through drama.

Resources

- 'Jabberwocky' by Lewis Carroll: www.jabberwocky.com/carroll/jabber/jabberwocky.html

What to do

1. Read 'Jabberwocky' aloud to the class. What do you think it is about? How can you gain a meaning when so many of the words are nonsense words?
2. Ask the children to close their eyes and then reread the poem to them, pausing when you reach certain words, e.g. 'Jubjub bird'. Engage in some thought-tracking (see Appendix 2), tapping individuals on the shoulder and asking them what image is in their mind – what does a Jubjub bird look like?
3. Explain to the children that they are going to prepare a dramatic scene, in groups, that represents what they think is happening in the poem (with or without words). Remind them that it is their own unique interpretation that matters – there is no right or wrong. Encourage them to talk in groups and decide the story they wish to tell and then to assign roles within the group.

4. Give the children plenty of time to produce their dramatic scene and then give them the opportunity to show their scene to the rest of the class (if they wish to).

Variations

- If the children find it difficult to create a whole scene from the poem, encourage them to choose a verse and then create a freeze frame (see Appendix 2) to represent this verse.

Cross-curricular links

Art – the children could represent the poem through art. This could start with a discussion centred around the nouns in the poem, e.g. 'toves' and 'borogoves', and the images that enter our mind when we hear these words. Children could compare their artwork, discussing how their representations of the nouns differ/are similar.

Word inventions

> The great thing about words is that you can make up your own! This activity allows the children to become word professors, experimenting in the laboratory of the classroom.

Suitable for

KS2

Aims

- To enjoy playing with language.

Resources

- 'Professor Frimpinsock' by Gareth Lancaster: www.fizzyfunnyfuzzy.com/showpoem.php?poemID=76

What to do

1. Tell the children that they are going to be word scientists, experimenting in the laboratory, creating new words of their own.
2. Read 'Professor Frimpinsock' by Gareth Lancaster. Discuss some of the professor's inventions – what do they think an 'Integrated Doodad' is? Or a 'Super-Tensile Jigger'?
3. If you could invent a machine to do a particular job, what would that job be? How about a bed-maker or a room tidier? What might these machines be called?
4. Ask the children to work in pairs or on their own to invent a machine and then make up a name for this machine, creating the strangest words possible. They might then want to go on to describe what happens when they start this machine. Is it a disaster like the

inventions of Professor Frimpinsock? Or are their inventions successful and likely to make them rich and famous?

5. Share some ideas and begin to think how they might be put into a poem.

Variations

- If you have time, before the children begin to create their own inventions and words, they could create illustrations to go with Gareth Lancaster's poem. This gets their creative juices flowing and might help them when they go on to be word scientists themselves.

Cross-curricular links

History – it would be fun to link this activity with looking at real inventions from the past and researching how they got their names.

Chapter 4
Poetry for all occasions

Introduction

There are many reasons to celebrate during a school year – saints' days, times of religious significance, days to celebrate family, changes in seasons – to name but a few. What better way to rejoice than by reading, enacting, listening to or writing poetry? Poems have the ability to say a great deal in just a few words and can be the perfect way to engage children with the concepts and sentiments involved in the occasion.

This chapter aims to provide ideas for poems to use and related activities, revolving around different events in the school year. Inevitably, within the scope of one chapter, it is not possible to include all of the many times during the year when celebrations take place, particularly with regard to the many festivals relating to different cultures and religions. However, it is hoped that the reader will be able to adapt particular ideas to suit a range of occasions, substituting poems where necessary, perhaps drawing wherever possible on the knowledge the pupils have about poetry relating to their own countries and cultures. As your pupils begin to realise that poetry is an integral part of any celebration within your classroom, you will soon have far more than the 15 activities I have included in this chapter. Before long, I am sure the children will be leading the way!

All of the activities in this chapter have been deemed suitable for both KS1 and KS2, but you may find that you need to adapt to suit your particular class.

Mother's Day secrets

This activity is based around the poem 'Present Smugglers' by John Foster. It is specifically about Mother's Day, but it is a narrative poem and could therefore be used to introduce this poetic form or just enjoyed for its subject matter.

Suitable for

KS1
KS2

Aims

- To recognise a family tradition.
- To empathise with others through poetry and the use of drama.

Resources

- Poems relating to Mother's Day: www.mothersdaycelebration.com/mothers-day-poem.html
- 'Present Smugglers' by John Foster
- 'Mum' by Andrew Fusek: www.poetryarchive.org/childrensarchive/singlePoem.do?poemId=6107
- A3 paper

What to do

1. Share reading of 'Present Smugglers' by John Foster. Make sure all the children can see a copy of the poem. Depending on the age and reading ability of the pupils, ask volunteers to read a verse each. What is the poem about? What is happening in the poem? Why is it called 'Present Smugglers'? Does anybody have a similar story to tell? Share stories with the class.

2. Draw a timeline on the board, showing the series of events that occur in the poem, so that the children are able to use this as a scaffold (you could use simple pictures or words to make this age-appropriate). The timeline might look like this:

   Empty money box → Buy scarf → Hide scarf under bed → Go to flower shop and buy plant → Smuggle into shed → Write cards → Wrap scarf → Give Mum presents

3. Divide the class into groups of four and assign roles – one person to be the mother, one the father, and two children. With KS1 children, ask them to re-enact the poem thinking about how the different people would feel. With KS2 children, ask them to draw 'emotion graphs' (see Appendix 3) on pieces of A3 paper to reflect the feelings of the different people.

Variations

- Hot-seating (see Appendix 2) could be used to portray how each person feels or how pupils in the class have felt in similar situations.

Cross-curricular links

Literacy – narrative poetry, focusing on time connectives and how these are part of the structure of the poem.
PSHE – how people might feel in given situations.

All about Dad

Although I have put this activity in to enable children to celebrate Father's Day through poetry, it could be used at any time of the year. Having selections of poems on themes at your fingertips is very important, e.g. poems about families, animals, seasons etc.

Suitable for

KS1
KS2

Aims

- To enable the children to celebrate Father's Day through poetry.

Resources

- 'Hair-raiser' by Judith Nicholls: www.poetryarchive.org/childrensarchive/singlePoem.do?poemId=394
- 'Daddy Fell into the Pond' by Alfred Noyes: http://heatheranne.freeservers.com/childrens/DaddyFellIntoThePond.htm
- 'My Dad Calls Me' by Michael Rosen: www.michaelrosen.co.uk/hyp_mydadcalls.html
- 'My Dad, Your Dad' by Kit Wright: www.schoolnet.org.za/conference/sessions/mn/JP%20Integration/Grade%202/Literacy/My%20dad%20your%20dad/Poem.pdf
- A4 paper with the outline figure of a dad

What to do

1. Ask the children to write down three words to describe their dad and share these words with a partner. Do you have similar words? Collect all the words from the class and record on the board.

2. Read the children a selection of poems about dads, discussing each one in turn, focusing on how dads are represented in each poem (funny characters, figures of authority etc.)

3. Read 'My Dad, Your Dad' by Kit Wright. If possible ask another adult in the class to help you, so that you read one verse each (the poem is told from two perspectives). Encourage volunteers to come and read the poem, in pairs, to the class.

4. Give out A4 paper with an outline figure of a dad. Ask the children to write words inside the outline that describe their dad's personality and write words outside the outline that describe his physical features. The children can use the words collected on the board to help them. These could be used as part of a class display, or they could be made into Father's Day cards.

Variations

● Children could think of a funny incident that has happened, involving their dad. They could use this incident to create a cartoon strip.

Cross-curricular links

PSHE – looking at families and the different roles that family members can play.

Christmas greetings across the miles

In this activity, pupils need to use reference books/websites/ knowledge of different languages from within their school to create a poem that consists entirely of Christmas greetings from around the world.

Suitable for

KS1
KS2

Aims

- To recognise that poems can be made up entirely of lists of objects/concepts.
- To identify Christmas greetings from around the world.

Resources

- Access to the Internet
- Reference/language books
- Multilingual dictionaries
- Christmas tree templates (see Appendix 4)

What to do

1. Read pupils a range of list poems: www.gigglepoetry.com/poetryclass/ bugshelp.html. What do all these poems have in common? They are lists, written as poems.
2. Explain the activity to the class – to create a class 'list' poem that celebrates the many different ways Christmas greetings can be expressed around the world. These greetings will then be added to a large, drawn Christmas tree, to form part of a display for the classroom (or school entrance/school hall). Children will then use their own mini templates, which they can then adapt for Christmas cards or in any way they choose.

3. Show an example that has been preprepared:

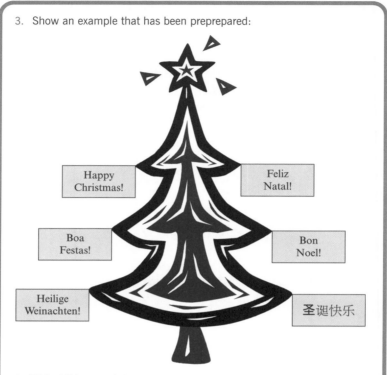

4. KS2 children work in pairs to complete research, finding greetings from around the world (a few pairs of children could go around the school, asking pupils and staff for their personal knowledge of Christmas greetings) and then adding their contribution to the class poem. KS1 pupils could work as a class, using the interactive whiteboard and websites, to find a range of greetings from different countries, which could be added one by one to the Christmas tree, forming a class poem. Children could then use this to create their own poems and use them for cards or other activities.

Variations

- This activity could be used at different times of year, e.g. Easter. For Easter, children could collect Easter greetings from around the world and then create a class poem inside the shape of an egg.

Cross-curricular links

Modern foreign languages – any opportunities to raise pupils' awareness of different languages and cultures need to be utilised. Some children will attend schools where there are many languages spoken and where cultural diversity is celebrated. However, there are also many children who have little experience of languages and cultures other than their own, and good classroom practice should seek to address this and provide opportunities for children to increase their knowledge and understanding.

Crazy Christmas

This activity gives children the opportunity to work together to produce a class poem. This takes away the pressure of working alone and enables children to listen to and absorb new and interesting vocabulary relating to Christmas.

Suitable for

KS1
KS2

Aims

- To create a class poem, using vocabulary relevant to Christmas.

Resources

- Selection of poems relating to Christmas: http://poems.christmas-presents-ideas.com/christmas-poems-for-children.html
- *The Young Oxford Book of Christmas Poems* by Michael Harrison and Christopher Stuart-Clark
- *Star of Wonder: Christmas Stories and Poems for Children* by Pat Alexander and Robin Lawrie

What to do

1. Read a selection of Christmas poems to the class, so that they are able to absorb the language and vocabulary. If you remember, ask them to bring in Christmas poem books they have at home that they can share.
2. Ask children to work in pairs to come up with as many words as possible connected with the Christmas season. Write these on a large piece of paper/whiteboard for children to use as a word bank.
3. Again working in pairs, ask the children to produce a phrase to describe a Christmas scene, using words from the word bank if they wish,

e.g. 'Crisp snow covering houses and trees'/'Parcels and packages, ribbons and bows'.

4. Ask each pair to write their phrase on a slip of paper. Collect in the slips of paper and then redistribute in any order. Give each pair a number from one onwards; when their number comes up, it is their turn to read the phrase they have been given. In this way, they will produce a class Christmas poem from all the phrases. After the lesson, these could be collected up in the order they were read, typed up and used as part of a poetry display.

5. With younger children, they could offer words or phrases that the class teacher records on the board; together, the class decides on an order to put these in, to create a poem.

Variations

- This activity could be recorded using audio equipment or a video recorder and the children could use this to assess their use of vocabulary and make suggestions for improvement.

Cross-curricular links

ICT – use of recording equipment.

Birthday bonanza

Most classes will have at least 20 children and birthdays will come around quite frequently. It is fun to celebrate with poetry. Here are some ideas that are quick and easy.

Suitable for

KS1
KS2

Aims

- To celebrate an occasion with poetry.

Resources

- Poetry anthologies with poems for each day of the year, e.g.

  - *Read me and Laugh – A Funny Poem for Every Day of the Year* chosen by Gaby Morgan
  - *Read Me Out Loud: A Poem to To Rap, Chant, Whisper Or Shout For Every Day Of The Year: A Poem for Every Day of the Year* by Nick Toczek and Paul Cookson

What to do

1. There are many anthologies that have poems for every day of the year. Once you have taken the register, it is a lovely idea to 'give' the birthday child their poem – reading the poem that is relevant to the date. This poem could be typed out or photocopied and put on a birthday display, which will be added to as the year goes on. If they wish to, the birthday child could write out and illustrate their birthday poem.
2. Many classrooms have 'message boxes' where children can put any notes to the teacher about issues they want to discuss; they might also be used for children to 'post' pieces of writing they have composed. When

it is someone's birthday, children could be encouraged to write poems for the birthday child and post them in the box, to be read out at the end of the day.
3. Don't forget that some children's birthdays will fall in the holidays; it is important to plan in advance to celebrate their birthday during school time, so that they do not miss out.

Variations

- Children often write accounts of the events that happen on their birthdays, or they are encouraged to tell the class about how they are going to celebrate. This would be fun to do in poetic form, particularly if a child has a party; the children who attended the party could write a poem to describe what happened from their own perspectives.

Cross-curricular links

PSHE – sharing experiences.

It's Divali tonight!

> Children love to find out about traditions and customs from around the world. Experiencing this diversity through poetry enables pupils to envisage the sights, sounds and feelings involved, in a way that might not be possible through other media. This activity could be adapted for other religious festivals.

Suitable for

KS1
KS2

Aims

- To recognise the significance and traditions of Divali, through poetry.

Resources

- A range of poems relating to Divali:
  - 'It's Divali Tonight' by John Foster: http://heatheranne.freeservers.com/childrens/itsdiwali.htm
  - 'Divali' by Joan Poulson: found in *Beware of the Dinner Lady*, an anthology by Brian Moses
  - 'Happy Divali': www.theholidayspot.com/diwali/poems.htm

What to do

1. If this is one activity of many that you are going to use to celebrate Divali, then the details of the festival may have already been discussed. If not, a brief discussion would be useful, to orient the children and to contextualise the poems.
2. Read a selection of poems relating to Divali. If you have children in your class who celebrate this festival at home, ask them to

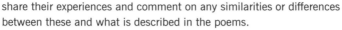

share their experiences and comment on any similarities or differences between these and what is described in the poems.

3. For KS1 children, printouts of the poems could be distributed for them to illustrate, selecting key aspects of the festival and portraying these through their artwork. These could form part of a display. KS2 children could work in pairs to find more examples of Divali poetry. These could be downloaded, copied out and illustrated to form part of a Divali display.

Variations

- If you have children in the class who celebrate Divali at home, ask them to talk through the celebrations they take part in. Record the events on the board, in the form of a story board. This can then be used to produce a class poem, celebrating this festival through the personal experiences of one or more of the children.

Cross-curricular links

Religious education – Hinduism.
Geography – customs, traditions and festivals around the world.
PSHE – awareness and celebration of cultural diversity.

Easter acrostics

> Acrostic poems are always good fun to have a go at and they make useful inserts to go into Easter cards. This is a quick and easy activity to make your children's cards unique to them.

Suitable for

KS1
KS2

Aims

- To use vocabulary relevant to a particular topic.

Resources

- Examples of acrostic poems. The following website has a brief introduction to acrostic poems and some fun examples: www.gigglepoetry.com/poetryclass/acrostic.html
- Coloured card or paper

What to do

1. Show the children some examples of acrostic poems and explain how they work.
2. Give the children five minutes to work in pairs and think of as many words linked with Easter as they can. Share these words and make a word bank on the board.
3. With older children, they can then work in pairs or on their own to write acrostic poems about Easter, using the word bank to help them. With younger children you might want to have giant letters spelling 'EASTER' pinned to the board and then work together to make a

giant acrostic poem, which could be used as part of a display. This could be photographed to go into their Easter cards or they could copy the poem.

4. If the children wish to, they can use their poems inside Easter cards to friends or family. If they are going to do this, they may want to design the front of their card to match the ideas in the poem, e.g. if they have mentioned eggs or chicks or if they have given their poem a religious theme, then their illustrations can be linked to these ideas.

Variations

- Acrostic poems can be made into real works of art, with children enlarging and decorating the initial letters that run vertically, deciding on fonts, colours, styles etc. If they are able to access computers, they could play with the text and find the best way to present their poems.

Cross-curricular links

Art and ICT – see ideas in 'Variations' above.
Religious education – Christianity, Easter.

Harvest around the world

This activity invites children to explore how harvest is celebrated around the world. They can then produce poems as a way of sharing what they have discovered.

Suitable for

KS1
KS2

Aims

● To recognise harvest traditions around the world and celebrate them through poetry.

Resources

● The two websites below give information on how harvest is celebrated around the world:

  ● www.teachernet.gov.uk/teachingandlearning/library/harvestfestivals/
  ● www.harvestfestivals.net/harvestfestivals.htm
  ● www.fleckney.leics.sch.uk/child/34hp.htm has a lovely alphabet poem written by children about harvest

What to do

1. Ask the children how we celebrate harvest in England. What are we actually celebrating? Explain that people celebrate harvest in different ways around the world. If you have children from other countries and cultures in your class, ask them if they are willing to share their own knowledge and experiences.

2. Use the websites above to find out about how different countries celebrate this festival. The children could select from the list of countries and you could make notes on a flipchart under headings ▶

of the chosen places – these could be related to customs, foods eaten, dances and songs etc.

3. Read aloud the poem written by a class of children about harvest (see website above).
4. Write a class poem based on the notes made earlier about a particular country's ways of celebrating. This could become part of a display dedicated to the customs and traditions relating to this country.

Variations

- If the children are confident writers of poetry, they could choose a country each (or in pairs or small groups), research the facts about harvest in that country and then write a poem. In this way, you would have enough poems to make up a display celebrating harvest around the world.

Cross-curricular links

Geography – knowledge of countries, traditions and customs.
PSHE – understanding and celebration of the different ways festivals are celebrated.

A bewitching time

This would be fun to do around the time of Halloween. It involves plenty of revolting objects and substances, so the children will love it!

Suitable for

KS1
KS2

Aims

- To create and sustain roles inspired by poems.
- To explore the use of onomatopoeia.

Resources

- 'Witches Stew' by Gareth Lancaster: www.fizzyfunnyfuzzy.com/showpoem.php?poemID=21

What to do

1. Read 'Witches Stew' by Gareth Lancaster. Discuss the language used to create the effects. What is onomatopoeia? This is where the word makes the sound associated with the object, e.g. 'gloop' and 'sizzle'. Ask the children to identify any examples of onomatopoeia in the poem.
2. Clear the classroom, so that you have a large space in the middle. Have all the children stand in a circle and explain that they are going to be a coven of witches, making a spell in their giant cauldron. As the poem is read, they are going to add the objects into the pot. When it comes to the part where 'spooky shadows dance around', have five volunteers who come into an inner circle and do a spooky dance with suitable sound effects. Ask the children to think of some other actions or moves or sound effects they could add.

3. Read the poem slowly and allow the children to take on the role of witches.
4. Explain to the children that they are all now going to add to the poem by thinking of one revolting object each that can be added to the cauldron. Their ideas will be inserted after the line 'Add the sole of one old shoe'; once they have added their ingredients, the poem continues. Give them a few minutes to think about what they will add.
5. Repeat the poem, with children adding their chosen ingredients and continuing with their actions.

Variations

- The class could write their own mini spells or potions and these could be read out as they encircle the cauldron. Alternatively, the spells could be written out and become part of a display with a large cauldron as the centre piece.

Cross-curricular links

Literacy – instruction writing. This would be an excellent opportunity to write instructions for creating a spell or a potion.

What am I?

This activity is based on the seasons – but it can be used for any season, so it is flexible. In fact, it would be great fun to repeat the activity throughout the year to build up a collection of poems.

Suitable for

KS1

KS2

Aims

- To vary writing to suit a particular purpose.

Resources

- Poems about the seasons. The following website has some useful examples: www.storyit.com/Classics/JustPoems/classicpoems.htm. Two useful poems from this site are 'An Autumn Greeting' (anonymous) and 'Buttercups and Daisies' by Mary Howitt

What to do

1. This activity can be adjusted to suit any season of the year. For this example, I shall use spring.
2. Read aloud some poems about spring, or ask the children to browse through anthologies to find some poems about this season. In groups, children produce mind maps with the word 'spring' in the middle, and all the words and phrases they associate with spring emanating from the centre. Encourage them to think about the sounds, smells and sights of the season.
3. Explain that they are going to produce a riddle about spring. This will involve describing the season, without naming it, and then giving their riddle to another person to solve.

4. Model an example. Here is one you might want to use:

I am a time of growth
A time of hope
Lambs frisk and play with me
I contain the month of April
I am not too hot and not too cold
What am I?
                    By Virginia Bower

5. Using their mind maps to help with vocabulary, ask the children to work in pairs or groups to produce riddles to which the answer is 'spring'. They can then go around to other classes and test them out.

Variations

● Rather than using words, the children could produce 'picture poems' – choose a word relating to spring, e.g. 'flower'; create a visual representation of a flower and this becomes the first line of the poem. Repeat with other ideas relating to spring and put one picture under another until you have a vertical group of pictures. Again, they can test these out on other pupils – what do the pictures represent?

Cross-curricular links

Science – nature and the seasons.

A spring in your step

This activity gets children outside – a vital aspect of classroom practice. Choose a lovely spring day and enjoy!

Suitable for

KS1
KS2

Aims

- To choose and use subject-specific vocabulary.

Resources

- Poems relating to spring – here are some examples:
  - 'Spring!' by Alex Fischer: www.poemhunter.com/poem/spring-197/
  - 'Spring Garden' by Gareth Lancaster: www.fizzyfunnyfuzzy.com/showpoem.php?poemID=37

What to do

1. Choose a lovely spring day (if you can!). Explain to the children that you are going to go outside and experience the feeling of spring. Ask them to think about what they can see, smell, hear and feel, relating to spring. They can either make written notes or pictures or just keep their ideas in their heads.
2. Return to the classroom and ask them to share their thoughts with the class. Make a note of any key words that arise.
3. Ask the children to take a few minutes to come up with one word or phrase that describes their experience when they went outside, relating to the season, e.g. 'fresh, light breeze', 'warmth', 'small, green shoots'.

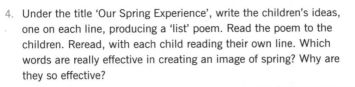

4. Under the title 'Our Spring Experience', write the children's ideas, one on each line, producing a 'list' poem. Read the poem to the children. Reread, with each child reading their own line. Which words are really effective in creating an image of spring? Why are they so effective?

Variations

- Spring tends to evoke the senses, so you could write a 'sense' poem, with each verse describing a particular aspect of spring in terms of the senses.

Cross-curricular links

Science – this activity could be linked with the human senses or lifecycles or other aspects of nature.

Summer recipes

This is a lovely activity to do just before the children break up for the summer. It will really get you all in the mood for relaxing.

Suitable for

KS1
KS2

Aims

- To broaden vocabulary and use words in inventive ways.

Resources

- 'Recipe for a Summer Holiday' by John Foster – if you put this title and poet into a search engine, and look for the books.google.co.uk link, you will find the poem there. It is also included in Foster's anthology 'The Poetry Chest'

What to do

1. Ask the children what they are hoping to do and where they are hoping to go in the summer holidays. Leave plenty of time for discussion.
2. Working in pairs, ask the children to come up with five words that they associate most with summer, e.g. beach, sunbathing, water parks, laziness, wasps. They can record these on mini whiteboards.
3. Read 'Recipe for a Summer Holiday' by John Foster. What has the poet done here? He has used the traditional format of a recipe – using imperative verbs, chronological order, adjectives to describe – and has created a recipe for what is needed for a summer holiday.
4. What would your recipe look like? What do you need for the perfect summer holiday?
5. Children can use the words they collected earlier to begin planning their own recipe for a summer holiday, and these could be used at a later date in their own poems.

Variations

- If the recipe idea is at first a little complex, the children could begin making list poems, based on what is needed for the perfect summer holiday. The poem would simply be a list of these things.

Cross-curricular links

Literacy – instructions. This would be a lovely and original way to introduce children to the linguistic features of instructions.

Autumn

There are many poems that have been written about autumn. I have chosen one in particular that focuses on frost and the effect this can have on the landscape, because I think it provokes strong images in the readers' minds.

Suitable for

KS1
KS2

Aims

- To relate a poem to personal experiences.

Resources

- 'Frost' by Valerie Bloom: www.poetryarchive.org/childrensarchive/ singlePoem.do?poemId=2812
- Icing sugar and a sieve
- Black paper
- Some images of frosty landscapes

What to do

1. Have you ever got up in the morning, looked out the window and found that the whole world has turned white? What might make the world go white? It could be snow or it could be frost. In the autumn it is more likely to be frost.
2. Read 'Frost' by Valerie Bloom. Give the children the opportunity to discuss how they feel about this poem. Reread the poem, asking a volunteer to pour some icing sugar through a sieve on to a piece of black paper as you read.

3. What happens to the black paper? This is the effect the poet is trying to create – to put an image in our minds of the frost silently laying on the landscape.
4. Look at some images of frosty landscapes. How does it make you feel? If you walked on the fields, what sounds would your feet make? Can you picture the air as you blow it from your mouth?
5. Reread the poem. Who is the giant? Is there really a giant who is creating the frost? The poet is using this image to create a particular effect for this poem. How effective is this?

Variations

- The idea of landscapes changing through the seasons could be followed up with art work. All the children could have a printout of the same landscape, and then they could change this according to the season they have chosen.

Cross-curricular links

Often topic work is based around the weather and seasons. Exploring these themes through poetry and art can be very exciting and rewarding.

Winter for me is ...

Most children love the snow and this is what they will probably mention first when you discuss winter. Therefore, this is a perfect subject for poetry writing.

Suitable for

KS1
KS2

Aims

- To use adventurous and wide-ranging vocabulary.

Resources

- Winter poems – here are some suggestions:
  - 'Falling Snow' (anonymous; Appendix 1h)
  - 'Winter' by Judith Nicholls: www.poetryarchive.org/childrensarchive/ singlePoem.do?poemId=397
  - 'First Snow' by Mary Louise Allen and 'Winter Arrival' by Marilyn Lott: http:// winterandkids.com/winter-poems/

What to do

1. Read a selection of poems about winter.
2. Ask the children to think of a memory they have of winter – it might be relating to snow or Christmas or sliding on ice – anything at all. Give them some time to think and then share their memories with the class.
3. Tell the children that they are going to write a class poem entitled 'Winter for Me Is ...' Ask them to write one line on their mini whiteboards about what winter means to them. Model an example, e.g.

   Walking through woods following snow tracks
   Or
   Sitting by log fires warming frozen fingers

4. Once the children have thought of their lines, put the poem together using their ideas. Between each line you insert, 'Winter for me is ...' so you end up with a poem that looks like this:

Winter for me is ...
Walking through woods following snow tracks
Winter for me is ...
Sitting by log fires warming frozen fingers
Winter for me is ...

Variations

- If the children are confident, they can create their own poems individually, using all their ideas and memories of winter under the title 'Winter for Me Is ...'

World Poetry Day

You need to have plenty of activities and ideas up your sleeve for World Poetry Day. Here are a few to get you started.

Suitable for

KS1
KS2

Aims

- To raise an awareness of the importance of poetry.

Resources

- Plenty of poetry books
- Access to the Internet
- Art materials

What to do

1. Have a slot planned for a morning and afternoon assembly. At the morning assembly, discuss the World Poetry Day theme and make some suggestions about how this might be celebrated. It would be great if all the classes could prepare a display and these could be put up in the hall or around the school. Children could link up with other schools via the Internet and discuss ideas and share poems. Poetry books could be created, using the children's own illustrated poems.
2. Explain to the children that at the end of the day, there will be another assembly, which will be a time to share the day's achievements. This might include some classes doing a performance poem or bringing the books they have made or reading some of their own poems.
3. During the day, try to visit each class, taking photographs and talking to children about their activities (I realise this depends on

having someone to help with your class, but perhaps you could ask a teaching assistant to take over for a short while and encourage parents to come in to support children).

4. Make sure that you publicise the children's World Poetry Day achievements. You could do this by inviting a member of the local press to visit the classrooms or attend the final assembly, or you could write up an account of the day for the school website.

5. The main thing about the day is that the children read plenty of poems and really enjoy what poetry has to offer.

Variations

I am sure that you will be able to think of many more ways to celebrate World Poetry Day, but here are a few more ideas:

- Invite a poet in to work with the children.
- Ask parents to come in to recite their favourite poems.
- Make audio tapes of children's favourite poems.
- Encourage the children to visit other year groups and read to/with them.

Cross-curricular links

Celebrating World Poetry Day enables you to include all different areas of the curriculum, depending on the theme and the activities you choose.

Chapter 5
Senses and feelings

Introduction

Many, many poems have been written about senses and feelings, probably because the poetry genre lends itself well to the use of well-considered, effective vocabulary, which is needed for people to express their own feelings or empathise with the feelings of others. This makes the theme particularly apt for the primary classroom, where children are beginning to discover things about the world they live in and to appreciate their place within it.

Reading and writing poems about senses and feelings links well with other areas of the curriculum, particularly music, art and PSHE. Being able to make links between other subjects and giving poetry a 'place' other than within literacy lessons, raises the status of poetry and makes it part of regular classroom life. This is soon accepted and appreciated by children, and you often find that they begin to make the links themselves, bringing you poems that they have enjoyed and that have some connection to something you have introduced.

This chapter includes activities that encourage children to put their senses to good use, making explicit what might be implicit with relation to what we hear, see, smell and feel. It also explores different feelings and emotions through the chosen poems and aims to promote useful and thought-provoking discussions that lead children to concepts they might not ever have considered.

The chapter contains seven activities that are suitable for both KS1 and KS2, four that are more immediately suited to KS1 and four for KS2. As with all the other chapters, these are merely guidelines and it is hoped that you might be able to adapt and adjust so that you can use as many of the ideas as possible.

Exploring emotions through poetry and art

This activity gives children the opportunity to explore a range of emotions and feelings and then to express their own ideas through art work and the use of colour.

Suitable for

KS1

KS2

Aims

- To recognise a range of emotions and feelings and to express these through the use of colour.

Resources

- A variety of poems relating to feelings and emotions:

  - 'It's Not the Same Anymore' by Paul Cookson: http://heatheranne .freeservers.com/childrens/ItsNotTheSameAnymore.htm
  - 'Mum Is Having a Baby' by Colin McNaughton: http://heatheranne .freeservers.com/childrens/MumIsHavingABaby.htm
  - Different-sized coloured and white paper
  - Art materials

What to do

1. Find a range of poems concerned with feelings and emotions (there are two ideas above). Read the children some examples, e.g.

   Joy
   Is a leaping gazelle
   Crossing the mind's meadows in a single bound
   Limitless possibilities
   The whole world
   Awaits

   by Virginia Bower

2. Group tables in the classroom so that each table has a 'feeling' or 'emotion', e.g. anger, joy, sadness, loneliness, fear. Have at least six poems for each table.

3. Ask the children to choose a feeling/emotion and move to the relevant table (choice is important here) and read the poems either with others or on their own (support from adults can be provided where necessary, although this should ideally be kept to support for reading the poems, rather than influencing ideas and opinions).

4. Have a range of paper and art materials prepared and ask the children to choose a poem that they wish to represent through a piece of art work, focusing particularly on the use of colour.

5. The poems and the art work could be displayed side by side.

Variations

- The children could select a poem as a whole class, discuss the feelings it promotes and then produce a large piece of art work to represent their ideas.
- Music could replace art and pupils could compose music to go with the chosen poem.

Cross-curricular links

Study the work of a famous artist, e.g. Van Gogh. Reverse the activity by producing poems from the art work, using Don Maclean's 'Vincent' as an example of song lyrics inspired by an artist. The following websites would be useful for this activity:

www.youtube.com/watch?v=dipFMJckZOM
www.myvideo.de/watch/6093247/Don_McLean_Vincent

Writing from experience

The more we can encourage children to write from personal experience, the better. Because their experiences will be genuine and unique to them, so will their writing.

Suitable for

KS1
KS2

Aims

- To explore experience through poetry.

Resources

- Poetry about people's experiences. Here are some examples:
  - 'At the Seaside' by Robert Louis Stevenson: www.storyit.com/Classics/JustPoems/atseaside.htm
  - 'The First Tooth' by Charles and Mary Lamb: www.storyit.com/Classics/JustPoems/firsttooth.htm

What to do

1. Choose a subject that you know will engage the children in your class. This could be linked with a topic you are studying or if you do this activity just after a break from school it could be linked with what they did on holiday. If possible, the subject needs to be relevant to all the children, so that they are able to draw on their own experiences. The two poems listed above are about 'typical' experiences – going to the seaside and losing a tooth – but you may need to find poems that are relevant to the subject you have chosen.
2. For the purposes of this example, I am going to use a trip to the seaside as the subject matter. Ask the children if they remember

their first trip to the seaside. Give them two minutes to turn to a partner and describe what they can remember.

3. Read 'At the Seaside' by Robert Louis Stevenson. Do they remember digging holes and making sandcastles? Discuss the children's memories and experiences.

4. Write out Stevenson's poem as prose in two sentences. This will show the children that to create a poem, they only need to think of two ideas, put them into sentences and then think about how they will present them on the page in poem format. Change the prose back into a poem, showing where the line breaks work.

5. If there is time, the children can write two sentences about their experience at the seaside and then change this into a poem.

Variations

- Haiku poems are a great form to use to record personal memories and experiences (see Chapter 6). They are short and very visual and children soon get the hang of writing them.

Cross-curricular links

This activity would be a great opportunity to link with other areas of the curriculum, whilst tapping into the children's own experiences. For example, if the children were writing about their memories of going to the seaside, this could be linked with history and how seaside towns have developed and changed over time.

Happy thoughts

In this activity, the children will produce one couplet each, relating to happiness. With only two lines to focus on, all the children should be able to produce their own mini poems.

Suitable for

KS1
KS2

Aims

- To use and adapt the features of a form of writing, drawing on their reading.

Resources

- 'Happy Thought' by Robert Louis Stevenson:

  The world is so full of a number of things
  I'm sure we should be as happy as kings.

What to do

1. Read 'Happy Thought' by Robert Louis Stevenson. What do you think Stevenson was thinking about when he wrote 'a number of things'? What would you say are the things that make you happy? Tell your partner three things that make you really happy.
2. Explain to the children that they are going to write their own 'Happy Thoughts' poem – just two lines long in the form of a rhyming couplet.
3. Model an example, e.g.

   Summer holidays, sand and sea
   This is what happiness means to me.

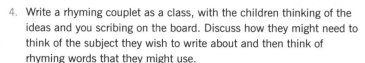

4. Write a rhyming couplet as a class, with the children thinking of the ideas and you scribing on the board. Discuss how they might need to think of the subject they wish to write about and then think of rhyming words that they might use.

5. Give the children time to write their couplets, providing support to those who may find it difficult to scribe their ideas. With younger children, they may wish to draw what makes them feel happy; they can feed back these ideas and the whole class can work on transforming their ideas into a poem, with you scribing.

Variations

- Once the children have created their rhyming couplets, these could be put together to make a class poem on happiness.

Sounds of our lives

Learning outside the classroom is a crucial element of school life. This activity encourages children to recognise and appreciate the sounds within an environment and to find vocabulary that reflects their experience.

Suitable for

KS1
KS2

Aims

- To recognise and distinguish different sounds.
- To develop a range of vocabulary to explain and describe different sounds.

Resources

- A4 paper

What to do

1. Take the children out of the classroom to another area of the school or to a local park or grassy area. Ask them to stand in silence and listen. Report back to their group what they could hear. If the area is suitable, ask the children to lie down, close their eyes and focus on the sounds around them. What could they hear this time?
2. On returning to the classroom, ask the children to sit with their talk partners and share their 'sounds'. They could make notes on mini whiteboards to help them to remember what they have heard. Each pair reports back to the whole class, whilst the teacher scribes key words on the board, discussing vocabulary and suggesting variations to broaden the bank of words the children can draw upon.

3. Give the children a piece of A4 paper divided into squares. Ask them to draw pictures or write words to describe what they heard, using a different square for each sound. Pupils can use the word bank on the board to support them with their task.
4. These 'sound squares' can form part of a display. The children could later write 'list' poems (see Appendix 5) using their squares to provide the ideas for each line of the poem.

Variations

- In their own time, the children could repeat the task, choosing a different environment, e.g. their bedroom/garden/a relative's garden. Again they could use 'sound squares' to record what they hear and bring these in to share with their peers.

Cross-curricular links

Science – sound/how we hear.
Music – pupils could use body percussion or percussion instruments to replicate the sounds they have heard in different environments.
ICT – digital recorders could be used to record sounds within different environments; these sounds could be saved on to display recorders (www .talkingproducts.co.uk/talking_tins_education.htm) and form part of the display with the sound squares.

Collecting sounds

This activity uses a wonderful poem by Roger McGough called 'The Sound Collector'. The activity I have suggested is designed to raise children's awareness of the sounds around them and links well to the previous activity – 'Sounds of our lives'.

Suitable for

KS1
KS2

Aims

- To raise awareness of sounds in the environment.

Resources

- 'The Sound Collector' by Roger McGough: www.bbc.co.uk/learningzone/clips/roger-mcgough-the-sound-collector-poem-only/8836.html

What to do

1. Ask the children to talk to the person next to them and describe five sounds they hear every morning any time between when they get up and when they leave the house.
2. Feed back responses to the whole class and discuss the range of sounds.
3. Access 'The Sound Collector' by Roger McGough on the website and play it to the children. Give them the opportunity to discuss the idea of someone coming to 'collect' all the sounds – how would they feel if all the sounds from their houses were collected? What would life be like?
4. Introduce the idea of 'sounds I would like to keep'. Ask the children to list ten favourite sounds (this could be individually or

as a class) that they would 'save' from the sound collector. They could then start a poem with the opening line

When the sound collector arrives, I shall save

and then use their ideas to create a 'list' poem, e.g.

When the sound collector arrives, I shall save
The scrunching of autumn leaves under my feet
The call of the first cuckoo in May
The whisper of the wind through summer corn

5. These poems could become the focus for a 'sound display'.

Variations

- This activity works well working with the whole class together. Each child can decide on the sound they would 'save' and a class poem could be produced, with each child adding a line. This could then be performed, possibly with accompanying appropriate sounds.

Cross-curricular links

ICT – using recording devices, children could 'collect' sounds from around the school. A poem could then be written, describing these sounds, and the poem could be performed with the recorded sounds playing in the background.

What is ...?

> This activity gets children to think about what makes something the way that it is, i.e. its characteristics – colour, smell, feel etc.

Suitable for

KS1
KS2

Aims

- To focus on subject matter and to convey appropriate detail to the reader.

Resources

- 'What Is Pink?' by Christina Rossetti: www.teachingenglish.org.uk/language-assistant/primary-tips/colours-what-pink

What to do

1. Read 'What Is Pink?' by Christina Rossetti. Write the questions on the board – 'What is pink?', 'What is red?', 'What is blue?', and underneath each question, ask the children for possible answers so that you have whole lists of possibilities to match the colours.
2. Choose one of the colours and an idea that the children have suggested that represents that colour. As a class, think of two lines of poetry (in the style of Rossetti's poem) to go with the colour and idea. Encourage the children to really think about how best to describe something so that the reader can picture it in their minds. Try to focus them on the most effective vocabulary, pointing out how Rossetti uses words like 'rich and ripe and mellow' to conjure up a picture of sun-kissed pears.
3. Give the children time to choose a colour and idea of their own and to write two lines relating to their choice. Explain that their lines do not necessarily have to rhyme, as rhyming can limit their word choice.
4. Share the children's lines of poetry. These could then be put into a class poem in the style of Christina Rossetti.

Variations

- This poem by Christina Rossetti lends itself well to illustrations. The children could each choose one of the colours and subjects in her poem and create an appropriate illustration. The original poem with the illustrations could then be displayed alongside the children's own poems.

Cross-curricular links

Art – recognising primary and secondary colours/colour mixing etc.

Chasing rainbows

This activity follows on well from the previous one – 'What is ...?' Again the link between poetry and colour and poetry and art is made, as children create their own rainbows.

Suitable for

KS1
KS2

Aims

- To collect visual and other information to help develop ideas.

Resources

- 'The Rainbow' by Walter de la Mare (Appendix 1i)
- 'Rainbow' (anonymous): www.starworldrocks.com/poems-for-kids.html
- A4 paper
- Art materials

What to do

1. Who knows the colours of the rainbow? Does anyone know how you can remember these colours? The children may well know some rhymes or songs to help them remember. If not, you could give them some examples, e.g. 'Richard of York gave battle in vain'.
2. Read the two poems about rainbows listed above. Discuss the different colours of a rainbow and perhaps access some images of rainbows online, so that the children have a clear idea of the different colours in their heads.
3. Give each group a colour and ask them to create a mind map with the colour in the middle and then any words, phrases etc. linked

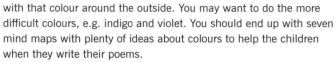

with that colour around the outside. You may want to do the more difficult colours, e.g. indigo and violet. You should end up with seven mind maps with plenty of ideas about colours to help the children when they write their poems.

4. The children now need to paint large rainbows on A4 paper, using wide bands of colour.

5. Leave the paintings to dry while the children create their own rainbow poems, using the words collected earlier (with younger children, you may want to create one poem altogether). Explain that they need one line for each colour, as they are going to write each line along the arch of each colour of the rainbow. When the paintings are dry, children can copy their poems on to their rainbows. These make a fantastic display.

Variations

- You could create one very large rainbow, which could span a wall space, and write a class poem to be printed out in very large font for all to see.

Cross-curricular links

Art – colour mixing.

Senses on the wall

This is a variation of the idea 'role on the wall' (see Appendix 5) and is essentially a fun vocabulary-gathering exercise, providing children with words to use at a later date.

Suitable for

KS1

Aims

- To use different senses when identifying a range of fruits.
- To use a range of vocabulary to 'put senses into words'.

Resources

- A range of fruits
- Outline templates of fruits
- www.clker.com/clipart-13230.html

What to do

1. Have different fruits in a bag and outlines of different fruits on the board. Ask a volunteer to put their hand in the bag and describe one of the fruits – how it feels – without looking at it. Other children can guess what it might be. Record any words that are mentioned within the outline of the fruit. Ask another child to take the fruit out of the bag and describe it. Any words connected with the appearance of the fruit can be recorded outside the outline on the board. Pass the fruit around and allow the children to feel and smell and continue to prompt for words to describe the sensations. These can be recorded inside the outline.

2. Repeat with other fruits, introducing where possible words and phrases that might be unfamiliar to the children (a great opportunity to extend and enhance vocabulary).

3. Have a range of outline templates ready so that the children can choose a fruit outline and begin to collect words of their own, using the examples on the board to help them.
4. In the next session, show the children a poem you have created from the words they offered that were stored within the outlines of the fruits:

Shiny skins
Hard and smooth
Crunchy and juicy
Dribbles down your chin!

By Virginia Bower

They might then go on to produce their own poems or work together to produce a class poem.

Variations

- The objects in the bag could be altered, depending on which sense you wished to focus upon, e.g. if the focus is touch and feel, then the objects might include cotton wool, a hair brush, smooth pebbles etc.

Cross-curricular links

Science – materials. Children need a range of vocabulary to be able to describe the properties of different materials.
Art – collage. Children could create pieces of art work that reflect the senses, using a range of materials.

Songs of the senses

With all children, but younger children in particular, it is important to make links between poetry and songs. The songs chosen for this activity are based on the senses.

Suitable for

KS1

Aims

- To identify songs relating to a specific topic.

Resources

- Songs relating to the senses:
  - 'I Hear Thunder': http://bussongs.com/songs/i_hear_thunder.php
  - 'The Five Senses Song' (sung to the tune of 'Old MacDonald'): www.preschooleducation.com/ssenses.shtml

What to do

1. Often songs and poems are related to our senses. What are our senses? Do you know any songs or poems about hearing or seeing or feeling? What about 'I Hear Thunder'?
2. Sing 'I Hear Thunder' if the children know it, or teach them the words and tune if they do not. What actions could we do to accompany the poem? Perhaps we should link these actions to our ears as this is the part of us connected with hearing. How could we represent the sound of the rain pitter-pattering? The children could use body percussion or percussion instruments. Sing the song altogether, with the sound effects and actions.

3. Read 'The Five Senses Song' as a poem and then explain that it can be sung to the tune of 'Old MacDonald'. Sing the song altogether and learn the words and develop some actions. The children could then visit the children in reception class and sing the song to them.
4. Have these songs as part of a collection of songs and poems on the senses. Encourage the children to find their own songs and poems to add to the collection.

Cross-curricular links

Science – the senses.

I'm so excited I could ...

Sometimes it is hard for young children to put into words how they are feeling. This activity gets them to explore feelings through ideas, words and actions, leading to poetry.

Suitable for

KS1

Aims

- To use language and actions to explore emotions.

Resources

- None needed.

What to do

1. What sort of expression might be on your face if you were really excited? Ask the children to show some examples. What do you do when you are really excited? Do you run around? Laugh and shout? Phone a friend to tell them how you are feeling? Ask the children to share what they do.
2. Give the children a scenario, for example they have just come home from school and their mum tells them she has just booked a holiday for the whole family to go to Disneyland. Ask the children to get into pairs and to role play this scene, with one child playing the mother and the other being the child receiving the news. How would they react? Give the children time to prepare their role plays and then show some to the class.
3. Give the children the line 'I'm so excited I could ...' and ask them to work in pairs to come up with an ending to the line. Model an example, e.g. 'I'm so excited I could burst like a balloon'. The children can either keep the idea in their heads or record on a mini whiteboard. Share their ideas.
4. Use these ideas in a class poem, where every line begins 'I'm so excited I could ...'.

Variations

- This would make an excellent performance poem, with the children enacting their idea of what they do when they are very excited.

Cross-curricular links

Drama – using role play to explore emotions.

Adverb action

This activity uses drama to explore feelings, with the added benefit of introducing children to adverbs and how they can be used to describe actions.

Suitable for

KS1

Aims

- To use language and actions to explore emotions and feelings.

Resources

- A list of verbs and adverbs

What to do

1. How can you tell how someone is feeling? Discuss facial expressions, actions, language etc. If someone was feeling very sad, what would their body look like? How would they be walking? What tone of voice would they use? How could you tell they were feeling sad? How might you react?

2. Tell the children that you are going to perform an action in a certain way, and they have to guess what you are doing and how you are doing it, e.g. 'skipping happily' or 'sighing sadly'. Model an example and then ask a volunteer to come up and have a go. Have a verb and an adverb ready for them to act out (begin with some easy ones as this can be quite a tricky activity at first).

3. Encourage the rest of the class to guess the verb and the adverb (you could introduce this vocabulary here if you want, but it is not vital that they know the technical terms at this stage). Ask them to explain how they were able to guess – was it the expression on the person's face or their actions or words?

4. Have a go at an adverb poem altogether, e.g.

   The boy laughed madly
   The girl sighed sadly
   The dog barked loudly
   The man sang proudly

Variations

- The children could do some research, finding verbs and adverbs that can be put together and acted out. They could test these out on their peers.

Cross-curricular links

PSHE – empathy and recognition of others' feelings.

A view of sadness

This activity looks at sadness from a slightly different perspective and will give the children the opportunity to explore the way language is used to portray this emotion.

Suitable for

KS2

Aims

- To identify words associated with a particular emotion.

Resources

- 'The House With Nobody in it' by Joyce Kilmer: www.poetry-online.org/kilmer_joyce_the_house_with_nobody_in_it.htm
- A4 paper

What to do

1. Read aloud the poem 'The House With Nobody in it' by Joyce Kilmer. Has anybody ever seen or been inside an abandoned house? How did it feel? What was the atmosphere? Has anybody ever moved house and experienced what it is like to pack away all their possessions and then walk around the empty rooms? Did you feel sad? Were you excited to be moving to a new house?
2. Give the children a copy each of the poem and ask them to work with a partner to identify all the words or phrases that have been used to create an atmosphere of sadness. They can highlight these words.
3. Feed back the words to the class and record these on the board. Are there any words or phrases in particular that really evoke the emotions?

4. Ask the children to divide a piece of A4 paper in half and explain that they are going to draw a house in each half. One of the houses is going to be a happy house, where there is lots going on, people laughing and celebrating, bright lights and warmth etc. The other house is going to be a sad house; perhaps it is abandoned or perhaps the people living there are sad or lonely. The children can choose how they wish to represent these two contrasting atmospheres – they might label the two houses, using appropriate words and phrases, or they might include colours and illustrations that speak instead of words.

5. Give the children plenty of time to complete this task and then share their work, discussing how emotions have been portrayed.

Variations

- The poem used in this activity could be the inspiration for a thought-tracking exercise (see Appendix 2). You could read the poem to the children and then ask them to close their eyes and imagine that they have just come across a deserted house, its doors and windows banging in the wind. They enter the house – what do they hear/smell/see/feel? etc.

Cross-curricular links

PSHE – to identify and recognise a range of emotions.

Feeling your way

This activity aims to introduce older children to poetry that expresses deep feelings. If the children are aware that writing poems can help people to cope with strong emotions, then they may find that they can turn to this outlet when they need to.

Suitable for

KS2

Aims

- To explore the way that poetry can help with strong emotions.

Resources

- 'Futility' by Wilfred Owen: Appendix 1j or www.bbc.co.uk/poetryseason/poems/futility.shtml

What to do

1. Explain to the children that people often read or write poetry to help them to cope with or celebrate strong feelings – whether this be love, grief, joy, excitement etc. Do the children know any poems that are about feelings or emotions? Share any ideas with the class.
2. Read 'Futility' by Wilfred Owen and then give them some time to discuss in groups what they think the poem is about. If they are not aware of the historical background, give them a brief outline of Owen's life and the way he used his poetry as an outlet for his very strong feelings in very difficult circumstances.
3. Reread the poem. Focus on the personification of the sun – how it 'touches' him and 'woke' him. How does this make you feel about

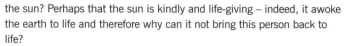

the sun? Perhaps that the sun is kindly and life-giving – indeed, it awoke the earth to life and therefore why can it not bring this person back to life?

4. Why do you think the poet wrote this poem? How do you think he felt – before, during and after writing the poem? Why did he give the poem this title – what does 'futility' mean?

5. Discuss how sometimes it can help to read or write or talk about feelings and emotions, rather than keeping them locked up inside.

Variations

- This poem could be used to introduce personification. The children could research poetry websites and anthologies to find more poems that use the same device. This could lead to poetry writing where they use personification to create a particular mood/effect.

Cross-curricular links

History – First World War.
PSHE – exploring feelings through poetry.

Guess the subject

The poem used in this activity really engages the senses and encourages children to think about how poets use words to activate our senses.

Suitable for

KS2

Aims

* To identify how language has been used to engage the senses.

Resources

* 'The Firebird' by Jean Kenward: www.bbc.co.uk/schoolradio/pdf/ storiesandrhymes_spring_2006.pdf (page 8)

What to do

1. Tell the children that you are going to read them a poem, but you are going to miss out a key word that occurs in all three verses. Children need to use the clues that lie within the language of the poem to guess the key word and thereby the subject of the poem.
2. Each verse of 'The Firebird' by Jean Kenward begins with the word 'fire' and this is the subject of the poem. Read the poem slowly to the class, missing out the word 'fire'. Give the children time to discuss in groups and record some of their ideas, keeping them secret from other groups.
3. Reread the poem, again missing out the key word. If the children are unsure, encourage them to think carefully about specific words the poet uses, e.g. 'smoky air' and 'ashes for a nest'. Give them time to discuss and then record their guesses on the board.

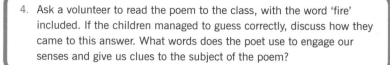

4. Ask a volunteer to read the poem to the class, with the word 'fire' included. If the children managed to guess correctly, discuss how they came to this answer. What words does the poet use to engage our senses and give us clues to the subject of the poem?

Variations

- The children could make a PowerPoint presentation to go with this poem, having a series of slides on a 'loop' that depict fire in its different forms, e.g. bonfires, log fires, forest fires etc. This could be played as the children read the poem aloud.

Cross-curricular links

Dance – the children could create a 'fire dance' to go with this poem. The poem has some wonderful words to inspire dance moves, e.g. 'leap and spring', 'fluttering' and 'sink down to rest'.

A tour of the senses

This activity, based on the poem 'Snake' by D H Lawrence, evokes all the senses. The language is fantastic and, although the children may not on first reading understand all the references, they can just soak up and 'feel'.

Suitable for

KS2

Aims

● To explore the senses through thought-tracking.

Resources

● 'Snake' by D H Lawrence: http://homepages.wmich.edu/~cooneys/poems/dhl.snake.html

What to do

1. Ask the children to close their eyes and then read 'Snake' to them. Try to read slowly, with plenty of expression and pauses, so that they can soak up the language and allow their senses to be engaged. Once you have finished the reading, give the children time to discuss.

2. Read the poem again, but this time introduce some thought-tracking as you go through (see Appendix 2). For example, read the first two stanzas and then ask the children to close their eyes and imagine the scene: 'You have walked in your pyjamas to collect water. It is a hot morning, the sun streaming down, the water shimmering. You are swinging your bucket dreamily, thinking about the breakfast you are going to make. You bend down to dip your bucket into the trough when suddenly you spot the snake. How do you feel? Does your heart start to thump more rapidly?' Tap a child on the shoulder and ask how they are feeling.

3. Move on through the poem, choosing moments to stop and use some more thought-tracking (it is a good idea to spend some time preparing where you are going to stop and the words you are going to use to engage the children's senses).
4. If there is time, give the children a copy of the poem and ask them, in pairs, to create an 'emotion graph' (see Appendix 3) of the poem – how did the person feel at different times during the poem?

Variations

• This would make a wonderful poem to perform, perhaps using musical instruments to create tension and mood.

Cross-curricular links

Music – see Variations above.

Chapter 6
Poetic forms

Introduction

One of the aspects of teaching poetry that concerns practitioners is their subject knowledge relating to the different poetic forms and the related vocabulary. It is a real pity if this lack of confidence leads to children missing out on the many types of poems that exist. I hope, in this chapter, to familiarise the reader with some common poetic forms and provide ideas for how children can read, share and write using a range of forms.

Five poetic forms will be explored – haiku, acrostic, kenning poems, limerick and concrete – and each section will have one activity that introduces the form, in order to familiarise the children with the typical characteristics, and then two other activities to further explore each form.

This introduction will provide some background information about the different forms and this can also be found in the glossary of terms (see Appendix 5).

The **haiku** originates in Japan and is often defined as being a three-line poem with 17 syllables set in a 5–7–5 format. This tends to be the first thing that children learn about this form and yet it is to some extent quite misleading, as the Japanese syllables are not compatible with English syllables. More appropriate would be 12 English syllables. Although it is useful for children to know this information, as well as about the history and origins of haikus, it should not dominate their thinking. Some children might want to challenge themselves to fulfil the syllabic requirement, while others may feel daunted and restricted by the format, so it is important to allow for flexibility.

A **kenning** is a compound phrase (usually two words) that describes an object metaphorically, e.g. a cat might be described as 'mouse catcher' or a chair as 'leg saver'. Kennings originated in Old English and Norse poetry and using kennings is a great way to introduce children to 'list' poems. Poems consisting of kennings encourage children to think about an object/animal/person and choose the best words to describe them, without completely giving the game away. Riddles are often made up of a series of kennings.

Concrete poems are more commonly known as 'shape poems' and are great fun to read and write. The idea of a concrete poem is that the layout is significant to the meaning of the poem. For example, if you were writing a poem about a very thin person, you might write a very 'thin' poem, with short words and lines that stretch more vertically than horizontally. The poem itself, therefore, becomes an image relating to the subject.

Limericks are a very well-known and much enjoyed poetic form. They have a very strict structure, with five lines and an 'aabba' rhyme scheme, and they tend to be humorous. There can be advantages to using limericks with children, in that they provide a predictable structure upon which young writers can model their own poems. However, they are surprisingly difficult to write, because of the 'rules', so you need to be aware of this if you are asking children to create their own.

Most people will have had a go at an **acrostic** poem. This form is therefore an excellent starting point for young poets. An acrostic poem consists of lines within which the first word begins with a letter, which, when read vertically, will spell another word. They can be very useful as mnemonics, where children use the poem to remember a particular word that is spelt out with the first letters in the lines.

An introduction to haiku

This activity provides an introduction to the haiku form and sets the scene for further activities relating to this type of poetry.

Suitable for

KS1
KS2

Aims

- To have an understanding of the origins of haiku poetry.
- To identify the features of a haiku.

Resources

- Examples of haikus:

  - www.kidzone.ws/poetry/haiku.htm – this has a useful introduction to haikus and some examples in categories, e.g. Spring, Easter
  - http://homepage2.nifty.com/haiku-eg/ – this site has some wonderful haikus written and illustrated by school children
  - Access to information relating to the history and origins of the haiku

What to do

1. Ask the children if they know what we mean by a haiku. Read them some examples. It is important that you read plenty of haiku poems, so that the children begin to absorb the tone, style and form.
2. Show the children the following website: http://haikuguy.com/issa/ If you subscribe to this, it sends you a haiku every day. Sign up and make sure that you spend a few minutes each morning sharing the daily haiku with the class.
3. What do the children notice about the haiku form? Discuss syllables, number of lines, subject matter etc. (see Appendix 5).
4. Where do you think haikus originated? Discuss the history and the origins of the haiku.

Variations

- Get the children to research this form for themselves, finding out about its origins and printing off some examples. This could be incorporated into a project for homework.

Cross-curricular links

Haikus are often written about nature, seasons, animals etc. so links could be made with science or art.

Guess who I am!

This activity involves reading plenty of haikus and having great fun at the same time. Children will begin to absorb the rhythms and style of haikus and this will help them when they write their own.

Suitable for

KS1
KS2

Aims

- To identify and recognise the features of haiku poems.

Resources

- Plenty of haiku poems:
    - www.kidzone.ws/poetry/haiku.htm
    - www.twodragonflies.com/bychildren.html

What to do

1. Remind the children of the features of haiku poetry – three lines; the numbers of syllables in each line; the fact that they are focused on one subject. Often haiku poems are written about an object or creature, but the object or creature is never mentioned by name, so you have to guess their identity from the clues in the poem. Read some examples (see the first website above) and see if they can guess the subject of the poem.
2. Check the form of the two poems about a frog and a kangaroo – they have three lines, the syllables go 5–7–5 and they are about specific subjects.

3. Read some haiku poems written by children (see the second website above). What do you think inspired their poems? What would you like to write a haiku about?
4. Encourage the children to start thinking of a subject for their own haikus, gathering ideas and words to use at a later date.

Variations

- There are many websites with examples of haikus written by children. If you have access to a computer suite, it would be useful to allow the children to explore some of these sites, selecting their favourite examples. In this way, they are being immersed in the form and are gaining ideas to use in their own writing.

Haikus are happening!

Because haikus are brief and can be about any subject, they are very accessible and not too daunting for children to attempt. After this activity, all the children in your class should have a haiku written by them of which they can be proud.

Suitable for

KS1
KS2

Aims

- To vary writing to suit a purpose.

Resources

- As many examples of haikus as you can find
- Photographs – your own and, if possible, ask the children to bring in photographs of family, pets, holidays, landscapes etc.

What to do

1. Go through the features of haikus. Remind the children that although some people like to keep rigidly to the syllable count, you do not have to (after all, our syllables do not match with Japanese syllables anyway, so we can be flexible!). I think this is very important, because children can become obsessed with getting the syllables correct, and then what they actually want to say in their poem becomes 'lost'.
2. Explain that the most important thing is to have a really good starting point – something that you feel strongly about and are interested in. Show the class some photographs that have a particular meaning for you – it might be an amazing shot of a landscape where you went on holiday or perhaps a photograph of you at a family gathering.

3. Describe the photograph and the background to it, e.g. 'I was in the Lake District and I climbed to the top of a mountain. The view from the top was stunning – the sun shimmering on the lakes; small dots that were people far below.' Write this description on the board.

4. Model how this description might be turned into a haiku by minimising the amount of words used, whilst keeping the ideas and the tone:

   A tough mountain climb
   Stunning views to lakes below
   People just small dots

5. If the children have brought in their own photographs, they can use these as stimuli for their own haiku writing. If not, they could think of a meaningful event in their lives, or something funny/sad/exciting they have experienced, and base their haikus on this. Make sure their haikus are published, either in a class book or as part of a display or perhaps sent to a website that publishes children's work.

An introduction to kenning poems

> Creating and using kennings to compose poetry is great fun and children soon get the hang of it. This activity introduces them to the concept of a kenning poem.

Suitable for

KS1
KS2

Aims

- To familiarise the children with kennings and how they can be used in poems.

Resources

- A range of poems created from kennings. You can find examples at the following websites:
  - 'Dad' by Andrew Fusek: www.poetryarchive.org/childrensarchive/singlePoem.do?poemId=6108
  - 'Mum' by Andrew Fusek: www.poetryarchive.org/childrensarchive/singlePoem.do?poemId=6107

What to do

1. Read 'Dad' by Andrew Fusek, but do not tell the children the name of the poem or read any lines with the word 'dad' in. Once you have read the poem, ask the children who the poet is writing about. Play the poem with Andrew Fusek reciting it. Repeat with 'Mum' by the same poet.
2. What is the poet doing here? Explain that if you describe something or someone in this way, it is called a kenning. Write the word on the board. Why do poets use kennings to make poems? Perhaps because it is a way of identifying and recording all the characteristics of an object or person in a concise way.

> 3. Give the children an example of an object or person or animal and ask them to think of a kenning that would be suitable for this. Model this first by showing a picture of a horse and giving examples of kennings, e.g. 'tail swisher', 'shoe wearer'. Children could work in pairs to invent some suitable kennings.
> 4. Share their ideas and note these down. They can be used at a later date when the children are composing their own kenning poems.

Variations

- Put a selection of kenning poems on a central table and ask volunteers to come up and pick a poem that they can read to the class if they are confident or that you can read to the class. Make sure they are poems where the subject of the poem is not revealed (like a riddle). Children can try to guess the subject in as few lines as possible.

Cross-curricular links

Art – kenning poems could be made into wonderful pieces of art work, with each child choosing a line that they would like to represent through their drawing or painting or collage.

Kenning chaos

> In order to be able to write their own kenning poems, children need to be exposed to many, many examples and then they need to begin collecting their own ideas. This activity prepares them for writing.

Suitable for

KS1
KS2

Aims

- To identify key words to use in kenning poems.

Resources

- Plenty of kenning poems. There are some good examples written by children on the following site: http://sites.google.com/site/smclibraryshaz/kenningspoetrywithyear2

What to do

1. Ask the children if they remember what a kenning is. If you have confident readers in the class, they could share the poems used in the previous activity – 'Dad' and 'Mum' by Andrew Fusek – to remind the class of the format of kenning poems.
2. Tell the class that you are going to do a kenning project, which will ultimately involve them writing their own (or whole-class) kenning poems. First, however, they need to decide on a subject and then collect ideas, words and phrases about that subject. Give them different ways by which to do this; for example, they could work in pairs and bounce ideas off one another; they could use the Internet to find out facts about their chosen subject; they might

collect pictures and photographs that they could use to inspire their thinking. If you have time to plan in advance, they could gather information and pictures from home.

3. Model this activity first. Choose a subject, e.g. flowers. Demonstrate how to create a mind map of words about flowers. Show them some pictures you have found that show flowers in different situations. You could then show them some kennings you have created, e.g. 'vase filler', 'people pleaser'.

4. Give the children time to collect their ideas and create their kennings. If they are ready, they could begin to put these together into a poem.

Variations

- With younger children, you may want to do this activity as a class, selecting a topic, gathering ideas and then creating kennings. If you can create plenty of kennings, children can then use these in any order they choose to write their own poems.

Cross-curricular links

ICT – one of the many ICT skills children have to learn is how to select from the vast quantity of information that is available on the Internet. This activity encourages them to focus their search on very particular areas and to refine their search accordingly.

Creating kennings

This is the third of three activities relating to kennings and is designed to give children the confidence to write their own kenning poems.

Suitable for

KS1
KS2

Aims

* To use kennings to create a poem.

Resources

* The following website below has poems written by children using kennings:
  www.michael-syddall.n-yorks.sch.uk/workfolder/kenningpoems.html

What to do

1. Show the children a range of poems written by other children, based on kennings. Discuss the features of a kenning poem.
2. Choose a topic as the focus of a class poem. In groups, ask the children to create a kenning relating to the topic (with younger children, you may need to support them with this).
3. Give each group a number and tell them that when you hold up their number, they have to say their kenning. Have the numbers ready on large paper. Make sure the table with the number one is ready. Each table in turn recites their kenning, and in this way a class poem is made.
4. Ask the children to repeat their kennings, one group at a time, giving you the opportunity to scribe the poem on the board.

Discuss how, by using different kennings in a poem, you can develop an awareness of a particular subject.

5. If there is time, the children can produce their own kennings on a subject of their choice.

Variations

- If the children are confident to write independently, they could produce their own kenning poems and then share with the class, testing their peers to see if they can guess the subject of their poems.

Cross-curricular links

Kenning poems can be written about any subject, so this activity could be used across the curriculum. For example, in science, children could write poems relating to specific topics, e.g. magnets; in this way they are extending their knowledge and understanding.

An introduction to concrete poems

This was always my favourite aspect of poetry to share with my class. This introductory activity gives the children plenty of scope to explore, enjoy and have fun.

Suitable for

KS1
KS2

Aims

- To introduce children to a particular poetic form (concrete poetry).

Resources

- Plenty of examples of shape poems. The following websites will get you started:
  - www.primaryresources.co.uk/english/englishC7e.htm#calligrams
  - www.literacyrules.com/concrete_poems.htm

What to do

1. Ask the children if they know what a concrete poem is. No, it is not a poem made of concrete! Explain that another word for concrete poems is shape poems, and they are poems that are written in a particular shape to represent the subject of the poem.
2. Show the children plenty of examples of concrete poems. If you have the opportunity, let them browse suitable websites that you have selected. When I introduce children to this poetic form, I put together a PowerPoint of different shape poems so that I can show it on the board and spend time enjoying and discussing.
3. Discuss the key aspects of shape poetry, i.e. the shape reflects the subject matter; the poems are usually quite descriptive, so that

the words match and support the shape; they are often full of imagery, e.g. similes and metaphors, onomatopoeias and personification.

4. Give the children some time to think of objects/subjects they would like to create a shape poem about and, if there is time, they could start to collect ideas for this project.

Cross-curricular links

Because shape poems can be about any subject, this poetic form can link with any area of the curriculum. They are often written about the natural world, which links well with science, and of course the very act of creating a shape poem is an artistic endeavour.

Concrete creations

Creating concrete poems is not always as easy as it looks. This activity provides children with a very strong scaffold to support them with their first attempts.

Suitable for

KS1
KS2

Aims

- To become familiar with the strategies for producing concrete poems.

Resources

- Examples of concrete poems
- Access to the Internet – at least one computer between two children, but preferably a computer for each child
- www.wild-about-woods.org.uk/elearning/concretepoetry/

What to do

1. Show the children some examples of concrete poems and discuss how they have been constructed and the features of this poetic form.
2. Go to the website above, which provides all the tools for creating a concrete poem. Model the activity, talking through your own thoughts and how you want your shape poem to evolve. Remind the children that they need to focus on two main aspects – what the poem will look like and the language to be used. Both of these need to support each other.
3. This site provides its own differentiation, in that children can either use the pictures and vocabulary provided, or they can

design their own shape and add their own words. When you model how the activity works, show both ways of doing this.

4. Give the children plenty of time to experiment with their own concrete poems; if possible, print these off. The children can then make their own classroom display or make a class book of concrete poems.

Variations

- If the children are very confident with this poetic form, they might want to work independently of the website, creating their own ideas for shape poems. It is important that they do not feel constrained by the suggested ideas.

Cross-curricular links

ICT – exploring tools on ICT programmes.

Shaping up

This activity gets children to think about objects relating to a theme and then to create their own shape poems on this theme.

Suitable for

KS1
KS2

Aims

- To use vocabulary effectively in a shape poem.

Resources

- Dictionaries
- Thesauruses
- Word banks
- Coloured paper

What to do

1. By the time you do this activity, the children should be very familiar with shape poems. Even so, take some time at the beginning of the session to share as many shape poems as you can find.
2. Decide on a class theme. This could be sport, weather, animals, school etc. Explain the activity:

   - Choose an object relating to the theme, e.g. for weather this might be the sun, snowflakes, wind etc.
   - Sketch the object – this does not have to be perfect at this stage.
   - List as many words as possible linked with the chosen object and write them next to or inside the outline sketch.
   - Highlight favourite words.

- Think about how the subject could be represented through shape – if the poem is about rain, the words could be written on a slant to show the rain lashing down. If the theme is sport and the object is a ball, they may want to write their poem as a spiral, inside the ball.

3. Give the children plenty of time to share their ideas and prepare their poem. With younger children, this might be better as a class activity – shared writing – with you doing the scribing.
4. The children could produce a rough draft, peer-review their poems and then produce a final copy.

Variations

- These poems could be produced using computer programs rather than paper and pencil. This could involve animation, sounds etc. to enhance the presentation.

Cross-curricular links

ICT – these poems lend themselves to the glorious wealth of programs available to enable children to present in different ways.

An introduction to limericks

Limericks are great fun and easily accessible. They have a very recognisable format and this provides a useful scaffold for children if they wish to write their own. This activity introduces pupils to the features of limericks.

Suitable for

KS1
KS2

Aims

- To identify the key features of limericks.

Resources

- There are three limericks read by Michael Rosen at: www.poetryarchive.org/childrensarchive/singlePoem.do?poemId=444
- A huge selection of limericks by Edward Lear at: www.nonsenselit.org/Lear/BoN/bon010.html – this is a great site because each limerick has a line drawing illustration that the children will love

What to do

1. Ask the children what a limerick is. If they know any, ask them to recite them to the class (as long as they are appropriate!).
2. Read a selection of limericks. What do you notice about limericks – what are the key features? As the children offer suggestions, write these on the board. They might include structure, rhythm, rhyme, syllables, the fact that they often begin 'There was ...'
3. Choose a particular limerick and ask the children to clap the rhythm for each line. How many syllables in each line? Which of the lines rhyme? What is the rhyming pattern here?

4. Discuss the tone and style of limericks – they tend to be funny, often silly and, certainly with Lear's limericks, nonsensical.
5. Ask the children to choose their favourite limerick from those that have been read. They could have a go at learning the limerick and reciting to the other children in their group.

Variations

- Find a range of suitable websites with plenty of limericks. Give the children the opportunity to research online, looking at the sites and enjoying the limericks. They could note down their favourites, perhaps cutting and pasting into a Word document so that they have their own collection to refer to at a later date.

Cross-curricular links

Literacy – limericks can be a useful tool for children who are learning to read. The predictable syllable number and the rhyme scheme give children the opportunity to really hear the sounds of words and to make informed predictions, even if they are not able to immediately decode certain words.

Guess the word

This activity reminds children of the predictable nature of limericks. This will be useful for when they have a go at writing their own.

Suitable for

KS1
KS2

Aims

- To make appropriate predictions based on rhymes.

Resources

- Plenty of limericks
- www.nonsenselit.org/Lear/BoN/bon010.html

What to do

1. Divide the class into four teams. Ask them to make up a name for their team linked with a colour, e.g. the Gorgeous Greens or the Brilliant Blues. Explain that you are going to read them some limericks, but you are going to miss out the last word of the last line. Each group has to try to guess the missing word and record it on their whiteboard. The team with the most correct answers will have their favourite limerick printed out to take home.
2. Have a selection of limericks ready – if possible have some easy examples first, where the last word is very predictable, and then move on to some more tricky examples, where there are several possibilities. Play the game.
3. Discuss why some were more difficult than others – perhaps where any number of words would have made sense. What made

it possible to predict? The rhyme and rhythm are the main reasons –
and of course the fact that it needs to make some sort of sense – even
if it is nonsense!
4. If there is time, the children could play the game in their groups,
having selected some limericks from books or websites.

Variations

- You could reverse this activity by missing out the last word of the *first* line,
continuing to the end of the poem and then getting the children to guess the
missing word, using the context and their knowledge of how limericks work.

Cross-curricular links

Literacy – reading. Prediction is an important strategy for children when they are
learning to read, and when they are working towards becoming fluent readers.

Writing limericks

Once children 'get into the groove' with limericks, and understand the typical rhyme and rhythm, they will undoubtedly want to write their own. This activity is designed to get them going.

Suitable for

KS1
KS2

Aims

- To write limericks, demonstrating an awareness of the features of this form.

Resources

- www.gigglepoetry.com/poetryclass/limerickcontesthelp.html

What to do

1. Access the website above. There is a list of instructions designed to take you through the process of writing a limerick and the features to look out for. You are then given a famous limerick to analyse, looking at the structure, rhyme, form, rhythm etc. This is set out in a simple, useful way and would not take long to talk through with the class.
2. Have a go at following the instructions altogether, creating a class limerick with you scribing. Make sure that the children are completely confident with the main features of this poetic form.
3. With older children, they could have a go at writing their own limericks and putting them into a class book of limericks. Younger

children could work in groups with adults (if you have adult support) or perhaps write two or three limericks as a whole class.

4. When the children have written their limericks, they could play the game described in the previous activity – 'Guess the word' – with their own creations.

Variations

● Because this poetic form has a very strong, distinctive rhythm, it would be good to record the children reciting existing (or their own) limericks and then play them back so that they become familiar with the particular characteristics.

Cross-curricular links

ICT – following instructions from a website. Audio-recording of poetry recitals.

An introduction to acrostics

Children love making up acrostic poems. This activity introduces them to this poetic form and gives them an opportunity to read plenty of examples.

Suitable for

KS1
KS2

Aims

● To become familiar with a particular poetic form.

Resources

● Examples of acrostic poems in anthologies and online
● http://college.holycross.edu/faculty/dhummon/acrostics/ submitted_by_children.html – this website allows you to access acrostic poems by children from all around the world

What to do

1. What is an acrostic poem? Ask a volunteer to describe what they think an acrostic poem is. Have an example ready to show the children, e.g.

   Cute
   Adorable
   Tiger!

2. Have poetry anthologies on each table that contain examples of acrostic poems and also, if possible, have an area set up with Internet access where the children can search for acrostics online.
3. Ask the children to use the resources around the room to find acrostic poems. When they find one that they like, copy it out

and practise reading it, preparing for sharing with the class. Give the children plenty of time to find, read, share and write out their chosen poems.

4. Share some examples with the whole class. What do you notice about acrostic poems? What do you have to make sure of when you are writing an acrostic poem? Encourage the children to think about appropriate vocabulary, using exciting words, making sure the words begin with the correct letter.

5. Go to the website above and look at acrostics by children from around the world.

Variations

*   You could have a range of acrostic poems waiting for the children on their desks and ask them to look through the poems and see if they notice anything about them (but do not tell them that they are acrostics). Ask if anyone recognises anything special about these poems and get them to explain to the class. This is a good way to get the children constructing their own learning, rather than you leading the session.

Cross-curricular links

Because acrostic poems can be about anything, they can link usefully to whatever topic you might be studying.

The name game

Using the children's names as a starting point for writing acrostic poems is always successful. At the end of this activity, the children end up with a poem and a book mark.

Suitable for

KS1
KS2

Aims

- To understand the features of acrostic poems.

Resources

- Examples of acrostic poems using people's names
- Coloured paper cut into the shape of book marks

What to do

1. Revise what we mean by an acrostic poem. Explain to the children that they are going to write their own acrostic poems, based on their own names. Give them an example, e.g.

   Jokey
   Amusing
   Never unkind
   Everybody's friend

2. Go through some tips for writing this sort of poem. First, the children need to think of as many words as possible that they think describe them. They can think about physical characteristics, e.g. hair colour, eyes, height etc. They also need to think about their personality.

3. Give the children time to draft their acrostic poems and then edit and redraft, after peer evaluation. Their friends may be able to provide some useful words and phrases to help them.

4. When they are happy with their poems, explain that they are going to use their acrostic poems to make their own book marks, which they will not lose as they will have their names on. Give out the coloured paper and the children can make their book marks.

Variations

- The following website acts as a scaffold for writing acrostic poems: www .readwritethink.org/files/resources/interactives/acrostic/. If you have access to a computer suite, the children could use this website to support them with their first attempts at writing acrostic poems.

Acrostics on a theme

Ideally, this activity will take place after the previous two activities in this section. By this time, the children will have a good understanding of how this poetic form works and will be able to concentrate on selecting the very best vocabulary for their own poems.

Suitable for

KS1
KS2

Aims

- To use adventurous and wide-ranging vocabulary.

Resources

- Dictionaries
- Thesauruses
- Topic literature

What to do

1. Depending on when you choose to do this activity, you could link it with different areas of the curriculum. Scientific acrostics would be great fun, making poems to go with topics such as forces, magnets, habitats, lifecycles etc. Equally, it would be great to link with history or geography, getting the children to think carefully about the vocabulary associated with different areas.
2. For the sake of this activity, imagine you have chosen the topic of geographical features. Children could choose rivers, mountains, valleys etc. as the focus for their acrostics. Model one yourself first, e.g.

> Running through countryside
> In and out of
> Valleys
> Ever flowing
> Reaching the sea
>
> By Virginia Bower
>
> 3. Give the children time to research their chosen subject – using a range
>   of literature, websites, dictionaries and thesauruses. Encourage them
>   to collect as much vocabulary as possible relating to their theme.
> 4. Allow time to write a draft, peer-assess, edit and redraft. These poems
>   could then be typed up and illustrated.

Variations

- If you could get the whole school interested in acrostic poem writing, each
  class could produce an acrostic linked with a particular topic and these could
  be shared in an assembly.

Cross-curricular links

Each time you begin a new topic, you could encourage the children to use the
new vocabulary they are discovering, within their own acrostic poems.

Chapter 7
Poetry all around us

Introduction

Children are unlikely to be unaware that they are surrounded by poetry; indeed, they are likely to associate poetry with 'something they do at school'. By pointing out to them that advertising slogans, graffiti, posters, shop names, song lyrics, playground games, raps etc. are all forms of poetry, we can open their eyes to the possibilities of this genre. Children suddenly realise that they not only recognise and relate to some of these examples, but are already engaging with them and are able to contribute in their own very individual and unique ways.

I believe it is vitally important that we make as many links as possible between school practices and what children experience beyond the school environment. By acknowledging 'poetry all around us', we are able to include the knowledge and experience children have gained in different environments, and celebrate this in the classroom through an exploration of poetry beyond that found in books and online.

In this chapter the activities involve looking at our known environment and finding links to poetry. This includes slogans, radio advertisements, party and playground games, pop songs, proverbs, posters and raps. The first 11 activities are suitable for both KS1 and KS2. Then there are two activities specific to KS1 and two for KS2.

Spot the rhyme!

This activity takes children beyond the classroom walls and turns them into 'rhyme detectives', whereby they become more aware and observant of the world around them and the language it contains.

Suitable for

KS1
KS2

Aims

- To identify how rhyme is used in different environments.

Resources

- Rhyming poems

What to do

1. Ask the children to define what is meant by rhyme. Read them some poems that rhyme and ask them to identify the rhyming words. Why do people write in rhyme? Do you like rhyming poems?
2. Discuss the use of rhyme outside the classroom, e.g. playground games/chants, advertisements, song lyrics. Give some examples of rhyming advertising slogans.
3. Make a class list of all the places/situations where rhyme might be found (this list needs to be saved electronically, so that it can be added to as the children bring their ideas into school).
4. Print off a copy of the list for all the children in the class to use as a memory aid. Ask them to take it away with them. If they spot any examples of rhyme being used at home or in any other

environment, e.g. shops, cinemas or shopping malls, ask them to record their findings and bring them into school.

5. Share any findings and add to the initial list. Discuss the effectiveness of rhyme and why it has been used in different situations.

Variations

- Focus on a particular area, e.g. playground games and chants, and identify the rhyme and how this adds to the entertainment value. The children could investigate throughout the school, finding examples from all ages and using these to make a school book.

Cross-curricular links

Literacy – one of the sub-genres within non-fiction is persuasion and persuasive writing. Advertisements are a useful tool when teaching this topic and this would tie in well with rhyme.

Slogan crazy

This activity follows on from and links in with the previous activity, 'Spot the rhyme!'. Here, the focus is specifically on advertising slogans and how these can be used to promote the effective use of rhyme.

Suitable for

KS1
KS2

Aims

- To identify how rhyme is used in advertising slogans.

Resources

- A 'bank' of advertising slogans
- Ideas from which children can write their own slogans (some ideas are included below)

What to do

1. Read the children a selection of rhyming advertising slogans. What do you notice about these slogans? They rhyme; they are very short and concise; they pack a great deal of meaning into a small amount of words.
2. Explain to the children that they are going to make up their own slogans for exciting new products. Give each group a sealed envelope. Inside each envelope they will find a product for which they have to create a catchy slogan, to attract buyers. Examples might be bubblegum that never loses its flavour, chocolate that makes you run faster, and gloves that make your handwriting neat.

3. Working in groups, the children open their envelopes and work together to produce a slogan to 'sell' their product, trying to introduce rhyme into their catchy phrases.
4. Share the slogans with the whole class, voting on the most effective use of rhyme and the slogan that is the most persuasive. Discuss how language has been used in a persuasive way.

Variations

- The children could make up their own products for which they want a slogan. They could seal them in envelopes and give them to other groups as a challenge.

Cross-curricular links

Art – the children could begin to develop art work to match their slogans, thinking about appropriate colours and illustrations to promote their products. Music – once the children have written their slogans, they could create jingle music to accompany the slogan, suitable for a radio advertisement.

Radio ads

Radio advertisements will be a part of most children's lives and they probably do not even notice them. Creating their own ads raises their awareness of the power of language and is great fun.

Suitable for

KS1
KS2

Aims

- To use language effectively.

Resources

- Examples of advertisements taken from newspapers and magazines
- Access to a radio to listen to a local station

What to do

1. What do advertisements try to do? They use persuasive language to try to get you to buy something. Often radio advertisements use songs or rhyming lines to catch people's attention. Why do they have to do this? What is the difference between a radio ad and a TV/newspaper/magazine ad?

2. Give the children the opportunity to look at some advertisements in newspapers and magazines and then listen to some on a local radio station. Explain that the radio ads have to last a certain amount of time and the advertiser has to pay so much per second – so they need to be short and catchy.

3. Give the children an example of an event relating to school, e.g. a summer fayre. If you were going to advertise this event on the

radio, what might you include in the advert? How might you persuade people to attend? Discuss the importance of using powerful, persuasive language. Ask the children to come up with some ideas for a radio ad.

4. Give them an example of one you have made up yourself, e.g.

   So much to do at our summer school fayre
   Saturday at 2 – you need to be there!

5. Have a go at creating an advert for a particular event/object – you could do this as a class or the children could work in groups or pairs, depending on how confident they feel. Share the results and present them as radio ads.

Variations

- Once you have created some radio adverts, the children could put them to music or create a tune to sing them to.

Cross-curricular links

Music – see Variations above.
Literacy – persuasive language.

Poetry in the playground

The children should be able to lead this activity, as they are the experts on rhymes in the playground. They may not, however, associate these with poetry and it is great to see them realise that, even though they weren't aware of it, poetry is a part of their lives.

Suitable for

KS1
KS2

Aims

- To raise awareness of the link between poetry and playground rhymes.

Resources

- A range of playground rhymes can be found at: www.woodlands-junior.kent. sch.uk/studentssite/playgroundrhymes.html

What to do

1. Ask the children to share any playground rhymes they know. If they are happy to sing/chant them, they could teach them to those who have not heard them before.
2. If it is possible, take the children into the playground and ask volunteers to demonstrate skipping or clapping games where rhymes are involved. Again, they could teach the others (you might be outside for the whole afternoon!).
3. If you make it back into the classroom with time to spare, ask the children to choose a favourite playground rhyme. Is this similar to other poetry you have read/listened to? If so, in what way? Discuss the rhyme and rhythm. Are playground rhymes different in any way?

4. Using an existing example, the children could insert their own words to personalise it and this could become the class playground rhyme. They could share this with other classes around the school and perhaps work with other year groups to produce a school collection of playground rhymes.

Variations

- The children could do a survey of all the playground rhymes they hear throughout the course of a week. These could be recorded/videoed and made into an electronic book to share with the rest of the school.

Cross-curricular links

Maths – data collection.
ICT – using audio and visual recording equipment.

Party fun

> The children will be very aware of games that are often played at parties. However, they may not realise that the basis for many games is a poem. This activity raises their awareness of this – you can have some great fun having a party in the classroom.

Suitable for

KS1
KS2

Aims

- To demonstrate how party games are often based on poems.

Resources

- You do not really need resources for this activity, although a knowledge of some party games and the poems upon which they are based would be useful, e.g. 'Oranges and Lemons', 'Here We Go Round the Mulberry Bush' and 'Ring a Ring o' Roses'
- www.woodlands-junior.kent.sch.uk/studentssite/playgroundgames.htm#12

What to do

1. Read 'Oranges and Lemons' aloud to the children. Do they know this poem? What do they associate with this poem? If the children mention that it is a party game, ask them to demonstrate. If they do not know the party game, teach them the rules (see website above). Play the game, with the words of the poem on the board to help them if they do not know them.
2. Do you know any other party games that are based on poems? Give the children a chance to discuss any ideas. Share their ideas

and offer some suggestions. Play some of the games, learning the words as they go.

3. These poems and songs are quite easy to remember. Why do you think this is? Discuss the fact that they are often in rhyming couplets and have a very clear rhythm and predictable rhymes.

4. If there is time, the children could think of a game that they play at school that is not based on a poem or song, and then make up a poem that fits the rules of the game.

Variations

- The children could visit another year group and find out what party games they play and explore whether these are based on songs or poems.

Cross-curricular links

ICT – the children could make recordings of the poems being recited and share these with another year group, encouraging them to play the game that is related to the poem.

History – party games and songs often have a long history, and it would be great to get the children to do some research into the origins of the games they play.

Locate the lyrics

If you read song lyrics as if they were a poem, they often sound very different from when they are sung. This is a fun game where the children have to try to match the words to the song.

Suitable for

KS1
KS2

Aims

- To make links between poetry and song.

Resources

- Words to well-known songs – these might be pop songs, hymns, carols. Here are a few examples:

  - 'All Things Bright and Beautiful': www.hymnsite.com/lyrics/umh147.sht – this has the lyrics and also the tune being played so everyone can join in
  - 'Angels' by Robbie Williams: www.lyrics007.com/ Robbie%20Williams%20Lyrics/Angels%20Lyrics.html

What to do

1. Explain to the class that they are going to play a game where you are going to read out some lyrics to a song, as if they were a poem, and the children have to guess the song. Put the class into teams of four or five.
2. Begin with an easy one, e.g. 'All Things Bright and Beautiful', but perhaps start mid-song, e.g. 'Each little flower that opens, each little bird that sings, He made their glowing colours, He made

their tiny wings'. If a group knows the answer, they get one point; if they can sing the song, they get a bonus point.

3. Pop songs are great to use, because they often sound very different when they are read as poetry. I have included a link to 'Angels' by Robbie Williams, which is a good one to use; it would be even better if you could have the song version to play once the children have had a go at guessing the song.

Variations

- Once you have played this game a few times, you could encourage the children to bring in the lyrics of their favourite songs and test the class by reading the lyrics as poetry.

Cross-curricular links

Music – this is the obvious link. It is a lovely way to share the children's favourite songs and get them talking about the links between poetry and song, lyrics and music.

Karaoke time

This activity could follow on from the previous activity, 'Locate the lyrics'. Here the children have the opportunity to perform their favourite songs. However, there is a twist – they have to perform them as poems, without music.

Suitable for

KS1
KS2

Aims

- To read aloud with confidence.

Resources

- You do not really need any specific resources for this activity, as the children take the lead and bring in their own material. It might however, be good to have some recording equipment, so that the children are able to listen to their performances.

What to do

1. This activity needs planning in advance. Ask the children to take some time at home to find a favourite song – this could be a pop song or a song they have learned at school or a family favourite. They then need to find and copy out (or learn by heart) the lyrics to the song. This could just be one verse or the chorus.
2. Explain to the children that they are going to perform their favourite song, but instead of singing it they are going to perform it as a poem, focusing on clear reciting with expression and thinking about volume and tone. Model an example, reciting your own favourite

song as a poem. Ask the children if it sounded like a poem or a song. Would they have known it was the lyrics of a song if you had not told them? This would be a good time to discuss the close links between poetry and songs.

3. Put plenty of time aside for volunteers to recite their poem/song. It is better if children volunteer for this, rather than choosing particular individuals. Some children may find it very daunting to perform to the class – others will love it! Those who do not wish to perform can lead the discussion following the performances.

Variations

- You could turn this into a game. Tell the children that you are going to read some lines aloud and they have to guess whether they come from a song or whether they are actually just a poem.

Cross-curricular links

Music – this is the obvious link. You could have some useful discussions about how, when lyrics are put to music, their meaning might seem to alter. You could also discuss how, when reading poetry without music to support, the importance of expression and tone is paramount.

Let's get lyrical!

Children love the idea of writing song lyrics, not realising that what they are doing is writing poems which might be put to music. Encouraging them to identify the place of songs in their lives raises an awareness of the links between poetry and music.

Suitable for

KS1
KS2

Aims

- To explore song lyrics and their place in our lives.

Resources

- A range of popular music
- Christmas carols
- School hymns/songs

What to do

1. Have some song lyrics prepared, taken from popular chart music, and read them to the children. Do they recognise the words and, if so, can they sing the song? If possible, have the song ready to play to them and encourage them to listen carefully to the lyrics.
2. Read the lyrics from a Christmas carol. What do the children notice about them? Discuss how they often rhyme and have a regular rhythm. What does this remind you of? Discuss the link between poetry and songs. Play the Christmas carol to the children again, encouraging them to listen out for the words that you read out.

3. Ask the children if they can remember any words of school hymns or songs. Ask volunteers to say or sing the words. What do hymns and school songs have in common? They are often depicting a message, and this is the same with pop songs – they are often about love and people leaving each other or different feelings and emotions. Discuss the power of song and how people write lyrics for a particular purpose.

4. Sing some favourite songs as a class and ask the children why they are so popular. Is it the words/tune/rhythm?

Variations

*   If you can plan in advance, it would be good to get the children to bring in their favourite songs/hymns/carols. If they bring in CDs, often the words are also included (you may have to 'vet' these CDs as some lyrics are not appropriate for school). The children can spend some time looking at the lyrics and how they are written, the messages they are conveying etc.

Cross-curricular links

Music – this is the obvious link. The children can have great fun composing their own tunes and writing the lyrics.

MFL – not such an obvious link, but if the children are studying lyrics, they could compare the lyrics of traditional songs from other countries with British songs and explore whether there are common themes.

Playing with proverbs

Most children will be familiar with a few proverbs. Some proverbs are like mini poems and can make good starting points for discussions on the use of language to make a point.

Suitable for

KS1
KS2

Aims

- To look for meaning beyond the literal.

Resources

- A list of proverbs: www.adl.org/tools_teachers/lesson_proverbs.asp
- A4 paper

What to do

1. Ask the children if they know any proverbs. If they are not sure what you mean, give them an example. If they know any, record these on the board.
2. What are proverbs and how have they evolved? Proverbs have a message and often mean something more than the literal words. Give an example, e.g. 'A friend in need is a friend indeed', and discuss the meaning behind the words. Go through some more examples.
3. How is a proverb like a poem?

   - They often rhyme.
   - They have a certain rhythm.
   - They are very concise.
   - They use language in a clever, effective way.

4. Give the children a list of proverbs and ask them to choose their favourite. Give out some A4 paper that is folded in half. Ask the children to copy out their proverb on one side of the paper and then create an appropriate illustration on the other. These would make a great display.

Variations

- The children could go 'proverb hunting' around the school, asking the teachers, and at home, asking family members. They could bring these back to the classroom to add to the collection.

Cross-curricular links

PSHE – often proverbs have a hidden moral, which could be used as a starting point for discussion.

Art – ask and answer questions about the starting point for their work.

Poetry throughout the year

The children will be familiar with poems and rhymes that crop up at different times of the year. Poetry needs to become high profile in your classroom, and drawing these seasonal poems to the attention of the children is a useful way of doing this.

Suitable for

KS1
KS2

Aims

- To link poetry and songs with events around the calendar.

Resources

- Poems and songs relating to events and seasons throughout the year, e.g.
  - 'Remember, Remember': www.rhymes.org.uk/remember_remember_ the_5th_november.htm
  - 'Christmas is Coming': www.rhymes.org.uk/christmas_is_coming.htm
  - 'Red Sky at Night': www.rhymes.org.uk/red_sky_at_night.htm
  - '30 Days Hath September': www.rhymes.org.uk/ thirty_days_hath_september.htm

What to do

1. The website above is very useful for finding rhymes and songs relating to particular times of the year. You will be able to access the words and lyrics, and there is also a brief description of the history and origins of the verse. Make a list at the beginning of the year of all the possible times you might be able to use some of these rhymes throughout the school year.

2. When you know a particular month/event is approaching, start to prepare a display that the children will add to. For example, towards the end of October, you could begin to plan for a fireworks and bonfire display. This might include accessing the site above and introducing the children to 'Remember, Remember'. They may well already be familiar with this rhyme, but they could learn it by heart and then copy it out for the display. You could share the history of the rhyme with them, and they may want to make up their own poems and stories linked with this historical event.

3. As children become familiar with the pattern of activities – preparing for a particular time of year; collecting songs, poems and stories; creating art work for a display; investigating the historical background etc. – they may well be able to take the initiative themselves and begin to bring in information from home that they have researched.

Cross-curricular links

History – this is the obvious link, as poems and songs have often been passed down over many hundreds of years. Children love to find out the origins of these rhymes, which are very familiar to them.

Enjoying the environment

This activity promotes an awareness of the local environment, leading to an exploration of this environment through poetry.

Suitable for

KS1
KS2

Aims

- To explore experience through visual image and poetry.

Resources

- Cameras and the resource to download photographs

What to do

1. Explain to the children that they are going to go out into their local environment – this could be the school playing field/playground/local park etc. – and take photographs of aspects of the environment that they find interesting. This might be a building, a tree, cloud formations, road signs etc.
2. Organise this activity so that there are enough cameras for the children to all take some photographs. This might mean going in small groups/borrowing cameras from different areas of the school/asking children to take photographs outside of school time and bring them in. If none of these options is possible, then you could take lots of photographs of the local environment and bring these in for the children to use (but this does not really have the impact you are looking for).

3. As a class, group the photographs under appropriate headings, e.g. our school, roads and cars, nature etc., according to the subject matter they represent. Choose a particular category and look carefully at the photographs, noting down the reasons the children took the shot and what the image means to them. Model how a poem might be written, based on the images, e.g.

Large oak tree
Its branches casting shadows over the grass
I sit in its shade, a relief from the sun
And think happy thoughts.

4. You could then choose to either write a poem as a class, based on a set of images, or – what could be better? – allow the children to use their own photographs to create poems.
5. The poems produced could be displayed alongside the photographic images.

Variations

- Instead of individual photographs, children could take video footage of different environments and this could be used as a starting point for poetry.

Cross-curricular links

ICT – using different equipment to record images.

Poetry for bedtime

Lullabies tend to have a gentle, relaxing rhythm and are often written in rhyming couplets. This activity draws attention to the fact that lullabies are poems with tunes and explores how they achieve their soporific effect.

Suitable for

KS1

Aims

- To explore how lullabies create their effect.

Resources

- 'Lullaby' (anonymous; see Appendix 1k)

What to do

1. Ask the children if they know what a lullaby is. Explain that a lullaby is a poem set to music that is designed to achieve a certain purpose – to send children to sleep.
2. Read 'Lullaby'. Ask the children to close their eyes and then read the poem again. Does it make you feel sleepy? It might not make you feel sleepy in the middle of the day, but it could do if someone sang this when you were lying sleepy in bed.
3. Reread the lullaby (or sing it if you feel confident). Ask the children to think about the way it is written – what makes it a lullaby? Discuss the way it begins with 'Hush, little baby', creating a calming, quiet effect immediately. Then you could look at the rhyming couplets and the repetition of key words, e.g. 'If' and 'Daddy's', and the effect they have. See if the children notice how the object at the end of

the second line of each verse is mentioned in the first line of the next verse. Talk about how all these devices are meant to send children to sleep.

4. Ask the children if they know any other lullabies that have been sung to them. If they know some, they could sing them to the class.

Variations

● When you have sung some lullabies to the children, ask them to think of words that they think make you sleepy. You could call these words 'quiet' words and make a list. You could then create a list of 'noisy' words and compare the words. These might be used later when the children are creating their own poems.

Cross-curricular links

Music – the children could use an existing lullaby and make up their own relaxing tune to go with it.

Rapping fun with KS1

Children are likely to be familiar with raps that they have heard on the radio or the television. They may even make up raps with their friends. Tapping into this will help raise the profile of poetry as the children make links with their existing experiences.

Suitable for

KS1

Aims

- To become familiar with the poetic nature of raps.

Resources

- 'Monster Rap' by David Holmes: http://learnenglishkids.britishcouncil.org/songs/monster-rap
- 'Cool Gray Granny Raps': www.granniesrock.com

What to do

1. Play 'Monster Rap', encouraging the children to join in when they become familiar with the chorus. This is a great multimodal text because it has the rap being sung, animations to go with this, and the words coming up on the screen. This makes it accessible to all the children, even if they cannot read independently.
2. Replay the rap and ask the children to think about how a rap is a type of poem. What poetic features does it have? It rhymes, it has a very regular rhythm, it has repetition etc.
3. Play 'Cool Gray Granny Raps', encouraging the children to clap along to the rhythm. How is this similar to the previous rap?

What do you like about it? With this rap, it has been written to teach us about the alphabet. Often raps are written to teach or to send a message to the listener. What message would you like to send out in a rap?

4. Using the rhythm and style of one of the raps you have listened to, the class could make up a short rap relating to something they feel strongly about.

Variations

• Teach the children the words to the 'Monster Rap', replaying it to them several times so they are familiar with the tune and rhythm. Turn down the sound on the video and have a go at singing along. This will reinforce the key features of raps and how they have a very distinctive rhythm and style. You will soon find the children 'rapping' around the classroom.

Cross-curricular links

Music – this is the obvious link. The children could have a go at composing or accompanying an existing rap.

Reading and spelling – the Granny Rap is all about the alphabet and has some useful spelling rules built into the lyrics.

Rapping moves for KS2

Raps will undoubtedly be considered 'cool' among your class. Exploring this form of poetry may result in you gaining the coolest teacher award!

Suitable for

KS2

Aims

- To recognise poetic features within raps.

Resources

- 'The Boneyard Rap' by Wes Magee: www.poetryarchive.org/ childrensarchive/singlePoem.do?poemId=382
- 'Talking Turkeys' by Benjamin Zephaniah: www.benjaminzephaniah.com/ content/235.php

What to do

1. Play 'The Boneyard Rap' by Wes Magee. Give the children time to respond to the rap. What do they notice about it? What do they like about it?
2. Replay the rap, encouraging the class to join in with the 'Wooooo!' Draw their attention to the one–two–three rhythm that goes with each line and clap this as the rap is played. Play once more, asking the children to clap this rhythm. As well as rhythm, what other features do raps have that other poetic forms have?
3. Read 'Talking Turkeys' by Benjamin Zephaniah. Is this similar to 'The Boneyard Rap'? In what ways is it similar and in what ways is it different?
4. Give each group of children eight lines of the poem to learn and encourage them to accompany their reading with body percussion

(or percussion instruments if they are available). Allow the class plenty of time to practise (you may need ear plugs!). You will have to do some lines yourself to fill in any gaps.
5. Perform the poem as a class, trying to keep the strong rhythm consistent throughout.

Variations

- Wes Magee's rap would make a great performance – the children could make skull masks and use percussion instruments to create sounds of the clicking bones.

Cross-curricular links

Music – this is the obvious choice. Raps enable children to focus on rhythm and there is no necessity to have expensive instruments. Body percussion can be just as effective and great fun.

PSHE – many raps contain messages that the poet wishes to convey. Benjamin Zephaniah has written many different types of poem. They often contain messages about subjects he feels very strongly about. These can be useful starting points for discussion.

Poster poetry

This activity encourages children to look at the environment around them and the messages that are being conveyed.

Suitable for

KS2

Aims

- To evaluate different formats, layouts and presentational devices.

Resources

- Examples of posters – films, supermarket products, events etc. These could be real posters you have collected, or examples found on the Internet.

What to do

1. Discuss posters and their uses. Why do people use posters? If it is possible, take a walk around the local area and make a note of any posters and how the messages are conveyed. If it is not possible to do this, you could encourage the children to take photographs or make notes when they go out with their families outside of school.
2. How are posters laid out? What format do they follow? What messages do they convey? Show some examples and encourage the children to critique them. Do any of the posters use poetry or rhyme within their message?
3. What messages are we trying to convey within our school? Gather ideas. These might include healthy eating, stop bullying or always try your best, or they might be informational messages about school events such as fetes, concerts or parents' evenings.

4. Explain to the children that they are going to design their own posters to convey a particular message. Somewhere on the poster they need to include some poetry, even if it is just a two line couplet, e.g.

   We are very proud within our school
   To have a healthy eating rule

5. Give the children plenty of time to design and produce their posters – they may wish to take them home to work on them.

Variations

● If the ICT suite is available, it would be great if the children could produce their posters using a suitable program. They could then play with font and image, editing and redrafting as they go.

Cross-curricular links

ICT – see Variations above.
Making posters that convey messages could be linked with many curriculum areas, such as science (healthy eating) and geography (global issues).

Chapter 8
Ideas to promote talk in the classroom

Introduction

It is widely accepted that children need opportunities to talk, discuss, explore through words, and listen to the ideas and opinions of others. In this way they develop their vocabulary and increase their knowledge and understanding of the world, as well as engaging in a social activity that requires responding to and obeying certain rules.

Current focus is particularly on 'talk for writing', and I would agree that it is essential to provide children with the time and environment to talk before they embark on any writing task. However, I feel that opportunities need to be provided for pupils to talk together where *discussion and the sharing of ideas is the end product*, rather than the focus being upon a written outcome. For this to happen, and to be effective, children need excellent and varied stimuli to give them something of worth to talk about. Poetry can be a useful catalyst in this way, promoting the exchange of ideas and opinions and providing the reader with perspectives they might not previously have considered.

This chapter aims to provide a range of ideas to promote talk within the classroom. Often the ideas may lead to drama and role play or writing, and could be integrated into a literacy lesson. However, the main aim in this section is to provide teachers with standalone ideas that engage the pupils in high-quality speaking and listening activities.

The first five activities in this chapter are suitable for both KS1 and KS2, the next five for KS1 and the last five for KS2. However, please look at them all and decide what is most suitable for your class.

What shape is your year?

This is a great activity to do at the beginning of the year, when you are getting to know your pupils and they are getting to know you.

Suitable for

KS1
KS2

Aims

- To discuss thoughts and feelings about the year ahead.

Resources

- 'What Shape Is Your Year?' by Clare Bevan (can be found in *Beware of the Dinner Lady*, school poems chosen by Brian Moses)
- A4 paper

What to do

1. Read the poem 'What Shape Is Your Year?' What is the poet doing in this poem? How do you see the shape of your year?
2. Ask the children to discuss in pairs/groups their expectations of the year ahead. What are they looking forward to? Are they worried about anything? Share any thoughts with the class.
3. Talk to the children about the shape of your year – is it the same as that described in the poem? Will it have lots of ups and downs or will it follow a steady curve?
4. Draw a picture/diagram to illustrate the shape of your year (when I have used this with pupils and students, some draw a wavy line, others an elevator – which sometimes gets stuck!).
5. Ask the children to draw the shape of their year and then explain their drawing to a partner.

Variations

- This activity could be carried out altogether – what shape do we see our year as a class? This could be drawn on a large piece of paper and, as the year progresses, events and experiences could be added, so that it becomes a kind of calendar that the children can follow as the months pass.

Cross-curricular links

PSHE – this activity enables the children to identify and discuss any worries they might have about the year ahead.

I used to think ...

We all have opinions and perceptions about people – and the opinions of children can be quite strong. This activity encourages children to talk about how they perceive others, and to question the tendency to make what can be mistaken assumptions.

Suitable for

KS1
KS2

Aims

- To use poetry to explore our perceptions of others.

Resources

- 'Who's Who' by Benjamin Zephaniah: www.poemhunter.com/poem/who-s-who/ (can also be found in Zephaniah's excellent anthology *Talking Turkeys*)

What to do

1. Give the children some examples of people in different roles, e.g. soldier, footballer, secretary. Ask them to describe how they picture these people (if there is time, they could draw how they perceive them) and write brief descriptions on the board to come back to later.
2. Read 'Who's Who' by Benjamin Zephaniah. What is the poet telling us? Why is he using this idea in a poem?
3. Go back to the children's descriptions/pictures. What do they tell us? Do we tend to have a certain picture in our head of what a policeman/nurse/poet/soldier looks like? Why is this? Is it to do with television/newspapers/video games/books?

4. Read the children your own version of 'Who's Who' (I have included an example below in case you need one in a hurry!).

I used to think cleaners
Were women
I used to think soldiers
Were men
I used to think teachers
Were boring
But I may become one of them!

By Virginia Bower

Variations

- Encourage the children to look in magazines and newspapers to see how particular people are portrayed, and then to discuss their findings with others.

Cross-curricular links

PSHE – it is important for children to be aware of how our perceptions can be manipulated by others. PSHE is a great time to explore these issues.

Shadow play

Using the wonderful poem 'My Shadow' by Robert Louis Stevenson, children can explore the concept of shadows and tell their own stories of how they have come to understand (if they have) how shadows are formed.

Suitable for

KS1
KS2

Aims

- To discuss personal memories and experiences.

Resources

- 'My Shadow' by Robert Louis Stevenson: www.mamalisa.com/blog/my-shadow-a-poem-by-robert-louis-stevenson-with-mp3/

What to do

1. Use the website above to play the children the poem 'My Shadow' by Robert Louis Stevenson. Make sure all the children can see a copy of the poem and then ask volunteers (if you have confident readers) to read a verse each aloud to familiarise the class with the content of the poem and the ideas Stevenson is presenting (if the children are not yet reading with confidence, read the poem yourself).
2. Discuss any unfamiliar vocabulary, such as 'india rubber ball', 'nursie' and 'arrant', so that the children are comfortable with the meaning of the poem.
3. Share an anecdote with them if you have one – perhaps a time when you have made shadow animals on the walls or you have

> tried to run from your own shadow as a child. Ask the children if they have had any 'shadow' experiences and share them with the class.
>
> 4. If you are teaching KS1 children, ask them to discuss in groups why they think the shadow suddenly disappears in the last verse. If you are teaching KS2 children, ask them to work in groups to come up with an explanation that they could use with younger children to explain the reasons why shadows come and go.

Variations

- On a sunny day, the children could go outside and record any shadows they see, made by different objects. They could then bring these observations back to the classroom and discuss their findings.

Cross-curricular links

Science – this obvious link would work very well. It is great to start a science project with a story or a poem, and this poem would raise some useful questions and promote the use of scientific vocabulary.

How do you eat yours?

When promoting talk in the classroom, it is important to find topics that children will enjoy discussing. Children love to talk about food and the ways they eat different foods, and I have used a very short poem in this activity to introduce this subject.

Suitable for

KS1
KS2

Aims

- To share experiences and preferences.

Resources

- 'I Eat My Peas With Honey' (anonymous; see Appendix 1I)

What to do

1. Tell the children the first line of the poem. What do you think about this? It sounds like a very strange combination of foods. Are there different foods that you like to eat which other people might find strange to put together, such as peanut butter and Marmite? Share favourite food combinations with the class.
2. Why do you think the person who has written this first line of the poem likes to eat peas with honey? Discuss the properties of honey – sticky, sweet, tasty, 'gloopy' etc. Tell the children that the key word here is 'sticky'.
3. Read the whole poem. So – why does he eat peas with honey? To keep them on his knife! What other combinations of food would

> be ideal together? What is often difficult to eat because of its size/consistency etc.?
>
> 4. Show the children an example poem that you have made up about a food that is difficult to eat. Here is an example that you might want to use:
>
>   *I eat my spaghetti with a straw –*
>   *It's good to suck, not chew;*
>   *Knives and forks are such a chore*
>   *But straws so cool to use.*
>
>   *By Virginia Bower*
>
> 5. Give the children time to talk about how they eat different foods.

Variations

- The children could discuss favourite foods and their most hated foods. This could lead to a discussion about personal preferences and how we are all very different.

Cross-curricular links

Science – healthy eating; the properties of different foodstuffs, e.g. salty, sweet, sour.
PSHE – tolerance of the opinions of others.

Getting along together

This activity encourages children to talk about the benefits of all getting along together and how this can avoid a lot of heartache.

Suitable for

KS1
KS2

Aims

- To extend ideas in the light of discussion.

Resources

- 'Two Little Kittens' (anonymous; see Appendix 1m): www.storyit.com/ Classics/JustPoems/twokittens.htm

What to do

1. Who argues with their brothers/sisters/friends/parents? What normally starts an argument? How is it normally solved?
2. Read 'Two Little Kittens'. What is happening in this poem? What starts the argument? How is it resolved?
3. Give the children a copy each of the poem and divide the class in half, with one half being the oldest and biggest kitten and the other half playing the part of the younger kitten. Reread the poem, with the children joining in with their particular lines.
4. How can arguments be resolved? In the poem, the kittens realise that it is much better to be inside, out of the cold, getting on together, rather than freezing and miserable outside. What other ways can quarrels be resolved? Give the children five minutes to work in

their groups to come up with some different ideas. Share with the whole class.

5. In groups, ask the children to use these ideas to come up with a very short role play scene, where there is an argument between two or three people that is eventually resolved. If there is time, show some of these role plays to the class.

Cross-curricular links

PSHE – resolving conflict.

Pattern spotting

This is a game to promote an understanding of how letters and sounds can be linked and to encourage children to understand how words sometimes disobey the rules.

Suitable for

KS1

Aims

- To explore the links and patterns between letters and sounds.

Resources

- Rhyming texts by Julia Donaldson, e.g. *The Gruffalo*, *A Squash and a Squeeze*, *Room on a Broom*

What to do

1. Read one of Julia Donaldson's rhyming picture books. What do you notice about this text? If the children do not mention the rhyme, prompt them and discuss how it is used.
2. Explain that you are going to play a game. Each group of children will have a sound pattern to remember, e.g. 'ight' in 'light'. When they hear this sound, they need to stand up, turn around and sit down again as quickly as they can. Give each group a sound pattern that occurs in the book and have a practice with one page.
3. Reread the text with the children joining in.
4. Choose a page in the book where there is an example of a sound being represented by two or more different spellings, e.g. 'grey' and 'pay'. Read the page and make sure the children can see the words clearly (on screen or a photocopied page). Ask them if they

notice anything strange. Discuss how sometimes letter patterns sound the same but are spelt differently.

5. If there is time, the children could look through more of Julia Donaldson's books (or other rhyming stories) and find similar examples.

Variations

● Once the children have got the hang of this game, you can make it more complicated. Ensuring that they can all see the text as you read, give them two or three different instructions, e.g. if they hear a certain sound they must clap once; if they hear a sound but see different spellings of that sound, they need to stand up and point etc. This can get very exciting so you may want to send them out to play afterwards.

Cross-curricular links

Literacy – spelling.

Playing with meaning

Poetry can show children how to play with the meaning of words. This activity encourages them to talk about how words and phrases can have a range of meanings.

Suitable for

KS1

Aims

- To explore different meanings for words and phrases.

Resources

- 'Hey Diddle Diddle' by Andrew Fusek: www.poetryarchive.org/childrensarchive/singlePoem.do?poemId=6109

What to do

1. Explain to the children that often words and phrases have more than one meaning, e.g. the word 'cheek' can apply to a part of your face (or bottom!), but someone who has cheek might be called cheeky. Likewise, the phrase 'Get out of here!' might literally mean telling someone to get out of a place, but it can also be an expression of amazement. Talk about the need to consider the context and the intended meaning behind the words.

2. Read 'Hey Diddle Diddle' by Andrew Fusek (or play the recording from the website above). This poem has lots of phrases that the boy in the poem misinterprets and is sure to make your children laugh. Reread the poem, stopping after each verse to analyse how the boy changes the meaning of words to suit him.

3. Focus on the final verse, where Dad says, 'Take your time!' and the boy takes actual time, in the form of clocks, and flies away

> with it. Discuss what is meant by 'take your time' and how it differs
> from a phrase like 'take your homework with you'. Because of the
> context, the words within the phrase take on different meanings.
> 4. These are quite difficult concepts for young children, but I believe it is
>   important for them to become aware of language and the power of
>   words at an early age. You could finish on a lighter note, giving
>   volunteers the first line of each verse to say aloud, with you reading
>   the rest of the lines. You could also ask them to be on the lookout for
>   other words and phrases that are sometimes not what they seem.

Variations

- Discuss with the class whether they have ever not understood what someone
  else is saying or have misunderstood and acted in the wrong way. Give them
  examples from your own life. Are there times when we deliberately do not
  understand?

Cross-curricular links

PSHE – children need to be encouraged to listen carefully to what others are
saying and to begin to think about how language can be used as a powerful
tool – to persuade, explain, question, describe etc.

Talking animals

Animals are always a useful topic when promoting talk in the classroom. There are many, many poems about animals and you could use any of your own favourites. I have chosen mine.

Suitable for

KS1

Aims

- To promote high-quality discussion.

Resources

- 'Cats Sleep Anywhere' by Eleanor Farjeon: www.moggies.co.uk/catpoems. html#catspoem
- Your favourite poems about animals/pets

What to do

1. Ask the children to pair up, ensuring that at least one in each pair has a pet. Tell them that they have to choose three words that best describe their pet. Give an example first, e.g. 'I have a cat and I would best describe her as lazy, cuddly and fickle' (try to use some words that the children will not be familiar with, thereby extending their vocabulary). The children can either remember the words or record them on a mini whiteboard.
2. Make lists on the board, under the headings of the different types of pet, using the children's words.
3. Read 'Cats Sleep Anywhere'. What does this poem tell us about cats? Has anyone got any stories about their cats and where they have found them sleeping?

4. Reread the poem. This poem describes something that is very typical of most cats – that they like to sleep and the more peculiar the place, the better! Ask the children what they think is typical about dogs that might be included in a poem, e.g. tail wagging, jumping up at people, stealing food etc.
5. In pairs, ask the children to choose an animal and think of three words that typify the behaviour of that animal – it could be a pet or a wild animal. Feed back to the class.

Variations

● The children could do an oral survey of the teachers in the school, finding out if they have a pet and asking them to describe their pet in three words. These findings could be brought back to the classroom and added to the word lists. These could be used later in poetry writing sessions.

Cross-curricular links

Maths – data handling is one of the topics that most classes will cover during the year. The children could use their findings and create a graph or bar chart showing their data. This could be extended into a whole class survey, finding out the most popular pets.

Mealtime madness

This activity revolves around a subject dear to children's hearts – food. I am sure that once you introduce the topic of favourite and most hated foods, you will not be able to stop them talking.

Suitable for

KS1

Aims

- To use role play to promote effective talk.

Resources

- 'The Fussy Eater' by Patrick Winstanley: www.funny-poems.co.uk/kids/family-poetry/f16-fussy.asp

What to do

1. Describe to the children your favourite food/meal. Include high-quality language, using this opportunity to extend their knowledge and understanding of a wide range of vocabulary. Ask them to turn to a partner and describe their favourite food/meal, using as many interesting words as possible.
2. Put the children in groups of four and explain that they are going to do some role play. One of the children takes on the role of a restaurant owner who is trying to persuade a family – mum, dad and child – to come into their restaurant and experience the wonderful food. The family members have to describe their favourite foods and try to persuade the owner to put these on the menu. Remind the children that they need to use interesting vocabulary to describe the food (you could have a word bank on the board to help them with this).

3. Model the activity, using another adult in the classroom if possible, so that the children are aware of the expectations.
4. Give the children time to work on their role plays, stopping them every few minutes to remind them of some useful vocabulary. If there is time at the end, the groups could show their role play to the class.

Variations

- The role play situation could change. It could be a family sitting down to dinner, with the mother and father trying to persuade the children to eat their sprouts/greens. It could be a market situation, with a stallholder trying to persuade passersby to buy their delicious products.

Cross-curricular links

Science – healthy eating. The children could consider the properties of different foods and have this as a focus of their role play – persuading people to eat healthily.

Questions, questions, questions

An essential aspect of talk and conversation is asking questions. This activity encourages children to ask relevant questions and listen to answers.

Suitable for

KS1

Aims

- To ask and answer questions relating to a particular topic.

Resources

- 'The Wind' by Christina Rossetti: www.storyit.com/Classics/JustPoems/wind.htm
- A4 paper

What to do

1. Read 'The Wind' by Christina Rossetti. Can you see the wind? How can you tell that the wind is blowing? What effect does the wind have? Divide the class into groups and give them a piece of A4 paper with the question 'How can you tell it is windy?' written in the middle. Ask them to develop a mind map with all different answers to the question, e.g. 'because people's umbrellas turn inside out', 'my cheeks start to sting'.
2. Feed back ideas to the whole class. Now reverse the activity – ask each group to come up with a question they would like to ask the class about a weather type, e.g. 'What tends to happen when it is very hot?' The children can record their question on a sheet of A4 paper and then pass to another group so that they can develop a mind map with as many answers as possible.

3. Feed back to the class. Reread the poem. What words are particularly effective in describing the effect of the wind? Ask the children to hand back their mind maps to the group that originally asked the question and encourage them to read all the different ideas.

Variations

- This activity can be carried out using different topics. It is better to choose topics about which the children know something already, e.g. family, animals, school. In this way, they are able to ask relevant questions and form appropriate answers.

Cross-curricular links

This activity could be linked with any other subject, as questions and answers are fundamental to the primary classroom. Subjects such as science and maths would really benefit from children being able to ask pertinent questions to extend their knowledge and understanding.

Spot the odd one out!

This activity encourages children to spot words that sound the same but are spelt differently. They have to spot the odd one out and explain why it is different.

Suitable for

KS2

Aims

- To identify spelling patterns in words.

Resources

- Rhyming poems that have words that sound the same but are spelt differently. The following website has some examples you might use: www.poemsource. com/rhyming-poems.html

What to do

1. Choose some of the poems by Joanna Fuchs on the website above. These poems contain words that rhyme and follow the same spelling pattern, e.g. 'night' and 'delight', and words that rhyme but do not follow the same spelling pattern, e.g. 'too' and 'debut'. Ask the children to identify these differences.
2. Explain that when writing poems, it is useful to have a bank of rhyming words that you can draw on and that words can rhyme even if they do not look as if they ought to. And vice versa.
3. Explain the rules of the game you are going to play: you will put up a list of words on the board and they have to work in pairs to identify the odd one out. This odd one out may look the same as the other words but will not rhyme with them. Alternatively, it will rhyme

but be spelt differently. When they have spotted the odd one out, they have to explain to their partner why it is 'odd'.

4. Here are some examples of word sets you could use:

rough, dough, tough, enough (dough is the odd one out)
tail, sail, nail, whale, fail (whale is the odd one out)
peer, ear, fear, gear (peer is the odd one out – you could also introduce 'pier')
wood, hood, should, good (should is the odd one out)

5. If there is time, the children could make up their own and test each other.

Variations

- You could have a competition, where you give the children a word such as 'night' and they have to write down as many words in one minute that rhyme with it. Extra points are given if they can find words that sound the same but are spelt differently, e.g. 'site'.

Cross-curricular links

Literacy – spelling.

The lost road

This activity uses the classic poem 'The Way Through the Woods' by Rudyard Kipling. It is a poem where much is implied but nothing is declared, and it provides an excellent opportunity for children to formulate their own interpretations.

Suitable for

KS2

Aims

- To use talk to explore 'between the lines' of a poem.

Resources

- 'The Way Through the Woods' by Rudyard Kipling (Appendix 1n)
- YouTube video at: www.youtube.com/watch?v=0aGIWYE5C0Q

What to do

1. Read/play 'The Way Through the Woods' by Rudyard Kipling. Collect the children's first impressions of the poem and record their responses on the board.
2. Discuss any unusual words – coppice, anemones, keeper, ring-doves, trout-ringed – and how the poet uses language to create his effect. Have some pictures or photographs to support some of the images in the poem, e.g. ancient woodlands, woodland flora and fauna (if possible it would be wonderful to link this with a trip to a wooded area or forest). The children need to be totally immersed in the sights, sounds and smells of a wood.
3. Reread the poem, asking the children to focus specifically on the second stanza, closing their eyes to enable their ears to really

> focus on the words. What do they think is happening here? Are there horses in the woods? Whose are the skirts that are 'swishing'? Emphasise the fact that you are not looking for 'right' answers – only their interpretations of the poet's words.
> 4. Ask the children to think about a different context – their school for example – and what sights and sounds might echo in the classrooms and corridors from past pupils and teachers. What 'school' sounds are likely to be captured within the walls? Give the children plenty of time to discuss this.

Variations

- This is a wonderfully atmospheric poem and could lead to some provocative thought-tracking (see Appendix 2), where the children are encouraged to close their eyes and imagine themselves in a particular environment and how their senses react to this environment.

Cross-curricular links

Science – woodland habitats, flora and fauna.
History – thinking about contexts such as woodlands or cities or schools, where many people have been and gone and events have occurred, and the effects this has had on the environment.

Atmosphere and image

Children need to be exposed to high-quality use of language and to recognise how powerful words can be. This activity focuses on how a poet can create an atmosphere and images in our head in just a few lines.

Suitable for

KS2

Aims

- To identify how poets create particular effects.

Resources

- 'Prelude' by T S Eliot (Appendix 1o): www.wsu.edu/~wldciv/
  world_civ_reader/world_civ_reader_2/eliot_preludes.html

What to do

1. Ask the children to close their eyes and listen to a reading of 'Prelude' by T S Eliot. When you have finished the reading, discuss any images that the words of the poem created in their head. What kind of atmosphere has the poet created? How does he do this? Discuss particular words and phrases, e.g. 'smoky days', 'grimy scraps', 'withered leaves', 'steams and stamps'.
2. Reread the poem. In what era do you think this poem was written? What clues are included in the poem? They might mention 'cab-horses' and 'the lighting of the lamps'.
3. If we were to write a description of a scene in twenty-first-century Britain, what would you make sure you would include to ensure that you created the right atmosphere and put appropriate images

in the readers' head? Give the children time to work in groups to decide on a place (city, countryside, seaside etc.) and ask them to create a mind map with the place in the middle and words and phrases all around that they feel they could use to create a picture of the chosen place.

4. Ask children to go on a 'classroom walk' to explore other groups' mind maps. Encourage them to make notes on any particularly powerful words that have created images in their head.

5. Share thoughts with the whole class.

Variations

- The focus could be on how the poem evokes the senses – the smell of steaks and smoky days; the feel and sound of withered leaves and beating rain; the sight of the lamps being lit etc. This is a very powerful poem and the poet's clever use of words appeals to all our senses, raising an awareness of the power of language.

Cross-curricular links

History – looking at different places and different eras and how the sights and sounds will have changed over time.

A twist in the tale

This activity aims to enable children to make links between traditional tales and poetry and to recognise that both genres can be subverted to entertain. This should give them plenty to talk about.

Suitable for

KS2

Aims

- To make links between traditional tales and poetry.
- To recognise subversion within the works of a range of authors and poets.

Resources

- A range of traditional tales
- Texts by Jon Scieszka/Roald Dahl/Colin McNaughton

What to do

1. Ask the children to retell the story of Goldilocks in groups.
2. What are the main points of the story? Share these with the whole class.
3. Read 'Who's Been Sleeping in My Porridge?' by Colin McNaughton. What is the poet doing here? Read some other examples where authors or poets have subverted a traditional tale (Roald Dahl's poems/Jon Scieszka's short tales in his book 'The Stinky Cheeseman and other fairly stupid tales'/Babette Cole's 'Prince Cinders'). Discuss as a whole class.
4. In groups, ask the children to pick a key line from a traditional tale, e.g. 'Who's been sleeping in my bed?' and change the line so that it is recognisable but subverted in some way.
5. Share lines and ideas.

Variations

- The children could prepare and present through drama a scene from a traditional tale, where they have made changes to the original text.

Cross-curricular links

Religious education – stories and poems play a part in all religions. The children could compare stories from different religions where the moral/theme is the same, but the details and structure varies.

Evaluations and comparisons

One important aspect of speaking and listening within the primary classroom is promoting evaluation of speech and identifying how speech and talk can vary in different circumstances. This activity explores this aspect through poetry.

Suitable for

KS2

Aims

● To evaluate speech and reflect on how it varies.

Resources

● The facility to listen to different poets reading their poems. The following website is useful for this (I have used two of the poems from this site as an example in the activity, but you might wish to choose your own): www. poetryarchive.org/childrensarchive/home.do
● 'Two Seasons' by Valerie Bloom: www.poetryarchive.org/childrensarchive/ singlePoem.do?poemId=1693
● 'Dusk, Burnham-Overy-Staithe' by Kevin Crossley-Holland: www.poetryarchive .org/childrensarchive/singlePoem.do?poemId=1502

What to do

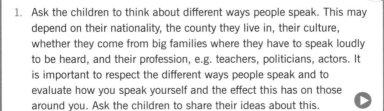

1. Ask the children to think about different ways people speak. This may depend on their nationality, the county they live in, their culture, whether they come from big families where they have to speak loudly to be heard, and their profession, e.g. teachers, politicians, actors. It is important to respect the different ways people speak and to evaluate how you speak yourself and the effect this has on those around you. Ask the children to share their ideas about this.

2. Play 'Two Seasons' by Valerie Bloom and 'Dusk, Burnham-Overy-Staithe' by Kevin Crossley-Holland. How do the recitals differ? What did you like about each of them? Was there anything you did not like? The children may not have been able to understand some of the vocabulary in the poems for different reasons. Did this affect your enjoyment of the recitals?

3. Ask the children to work in pairs to choose a favourite poem each and then recite the poem to each other. Encourage them to evaluate themselves and the other person, giving one piece of positive feedback and one area for improvement.

4. If any of the children are confident enough to give a recital to the whole class, this could lead to some useful evaluation. Follow this with a discussion reiterating the fact that speech varies according to a number of factors.

Variations

- Instead of choosing different poems, each pair could have the same poem and could present this to the class. Evaluations and comparisons could be made regarding the different ways the children have presented the poem.

Cross-curricular links

PSHE – raising an awareness of difference and the importance of respecting the different ways by which people express themselves.

Chapter 9
Ideas to promote reading in the classroom

Introduction

All the time, as teachers, we are trying to ensure that children are engaged with their learning. We strive constantly to find ways to stimulate their imagination and make them thirsty for more knowledge. Promoting reading in the classroom – for pleasure, entertainment, knowledge, shared emotions and experiences – is one way of achieving this. Promoting *poetry* reading has advantages that are specific to this genre and make it an inclusive and accessible activity. The advantages are that most poems can be read and enjoyed in one sitting – they are not like novels, which might take days, weeks or months to finish; they are not like picture books, where attention is divided between visual image and text; they are not like films or plays, where time is needed to watch the whole production. Poems do, however, have the ability to do everything these other genres do, and more. They can make you laugh or cry; they can provide facts or fantasy; they can transport the reader to other worlds; they can relate to you in the reality of your own world. Poems can create pictures in the reader's mind as effectively as a picture book or film, and they can describe a setting, character or emotion as vividly as a novel or short story. Their power is immense, and children need to be made aware of this power in order to use it for their own purposes.

Having said all this, there is a more pragmatic aspect to using poetry in the primary classroom. Poems help to teach children to read, to develop fluent readers and to produce critical readers who are prepared to question, hypothesise and argue. Although I feel that the most important aspect of teaching using poetry is to promote pleasure and enjoyment, there is no doubt that many of the objectives and outcomes that are part and parcel of everyday planning and teaching can be met through poetry, while retaining the fun element. I have, therefore, divided this chapter to try to accommodate all of these aspects.

The chapter begins with five ideas to promote a real enjoyment of reading poetry; the activities are designed to be able to be adapted for both KS1 and KS2. This is followed by five ideas specifically for KS1, focusing on using poetry to help with both decoding and comprehension. Finally there are five ideas for KS2, focusing on spelling patterns, and different strategies to promote fluent reading and inference and deduction.

Poetry, poetry, everywhere!

This activity is ideal to use at the beginning of a unit of work on poetry. It is also an excellent way to get to know your class and can be used in the first few days of the new term.

Suitable for

KS1
KS2

Aims

- To familiarise children with a wide range of poems.
- To encourage children to express opinions and to explain why they like or dislike a particular poem.

Resources

- A wide range of poetry books
- Computers showing poetry websites
- Nursery rhymes, songs and recorded poems for younger children
- Toys that, when a button is pressed for example, a poem or nursery rhyme is played

What to do

1. Have areas set up around the classroom where poems are available to be read and shared. This could include a comfortable space with cushions, an area with access to computers, a corner with audio equipment, and tables with toys and games that involve poetry or rhymes.
2. Model the activity: go to an area and find a poem that you like, perhaps read out loud to the class, and then move on to another area and show them how the equipment works. Make sure that

they are aware that they are free to read poems to themselves, to each other, to other adults in the room or to just listen to poems if they are in an area where this is possible.

3. Children can explore the room – you could set up a carousel – having an opportunity to visit each area. Depending on the age and experience of the children, you might want to make some suggestions, e.g. if you find a poem that you particularly like, try to remember the title or the poet so that we can all share it later; if you would like to read a poem aloud to someone, find a friend or ask an adult. It is very important that you are part of the activity – you are modelling reading poems or listening to poems being read.

4. When everyone has had an opportunity to explore each area, bring the children back together and ask if anybody would like to share a poem they enjoyed – either they could read it or you could take over the reading. Encourage the children to articulate their preferences and why they particularly liked a certain poem.

Variations

- Once the children are familiar with this activity, you could be more specific with your choice of poetry; for example, if you are intending to study haikus or concrete poems, you could select only these forms.

Cross-curricular links

PSHE – being able to state preferences and justify them; listening to others' opinions.

Pick a poet

This activity gives children the opportunity to immerse themselves within the work of a chosen poet and to find out about the poet as a person and what inspires them to write poetry.

Suitable for

KS1
KS2

Aims

- To become familiar with the style of a particular poet.
- To understand what inspires people to write poetry.

Resources

- www.poetryarchive.org/childrensarchive/home.do
- Anthologies

What to do

1. Read the children a selection of poems by a chosen poet, e.g. Brian Moses, Michael Rosen, Spike Milligan, Brian Patten, Colin McNaughton, John Foster, Benjamin Zephaniah, Allan Ahlberg, Valerie Bloom or Judith Nicholls. Are there any similarities within the poems? Do the poets tend to write about particular subjects or in a certain style?
2. Explain to the children that they are going to carry out a 'poet study' (this could be individually, in pairs or in groups, depending on age/ability/time). This will involve choosing a poet, reading/listening to a good selection of their poems and finding out about their lives/habits/pets/hobbies/interests and their motivation for writing poetry.

3. Show the children a range of websites that would be useful for gathering information (see Appendix 6). Even if the children are non-readers, they can be shown how to access poems that can be played and listened to. Websites such as the Poetry Archive also have recorded interviews with poets, so the children do not necessarily have to be confident readers in order to gather facts.

4. This could be an ongoing project, where the children continue to build on their knowledge of the poets and their poems. This information could become part of a display/class book.

Variations

- This activity could be promoted throughout the school, with each class choosing a poet to research. The hall could be used to display some of the poems and facts. This would be a great whole-day activity for World Poetry Day and encourages an interest in poetry for the entire school community (parents could be invited in to help with the research/creating displays).

Cross-curricular links

Inevitably, as children choose different poets and poems, there will be links made with other areas of the curriculum. Often poets write on certain themes, e.g. animals, seasons or war, and teachers need to grasp any opportunities to make connections with topics being studied or that will be studied later in the year.

Poem share

It is your duty to promote a love of poetry reading throughout the school. This activity is a step towards achieving this.

Suitable for

KS1
KS2

Aims

- To present to different audiences.

Resources

- Poetry books and anthologies
- Poetry websites (see Appendix 6)

What to do

1. Explain to your class that they are going to be ambassadors for poetry in the school. This means that they need to find a poem that they really love, practise reading this poem and then, if they are confident, share this poem with a child from another class or perform it to a class. They need to consider the age group they will be addressing to ensure that the poem choice is appropriate.
2. For younger children you may want to read some poems altogether and then choose some poems for them to practise (again this could be done as a class rather than individually). With older children, they could be left to read and select their own favourites and work in pairs, practising and helping each other towards a polished performance.

3. Practise within the class, focusing on clarity of recital, annunciation, volume etc. This would be a good opportunity for children to peer- and self-evaluate. Most children are familiar with three stars and a wish – they decide on three aspects they think are particularly good and one thing that could be improved – and this would be a good way to encourage children to make improvements to their performances.
4. Take your 'poetry circus' around the school. When you return to the classroom, encourage the children to share their experiences.

Variations

- This could be promoted as a whole school activity. A morning could be spent preparing, and the afternoon spent with children visiting different classes and sharing their favourite poems.

Cross-curricular links

This activity could be themed, according to different subjects. For example, each class could choose poems linked with a science/history/geography project.

Poem share at home

This activity leads on from the previous one, taking the idea from the classroom into the children's homes.

Suitable for

KS1
KS2

Aims

- To share ideas and experiences.

Resources

- Poetry books and anthologies
- Poetry websites (see Appendix 6)

What to do

1. Inform the children's parents in advance that the children are involved in a poetry project and that they are going to be coming home with different poems to share with the family. Ask them to let you know if they would be prepared to come in and read some of *their* favourite poems to the children.
2. Read plenty of poems to the class and give them the opportunity to read in groups or alone, selecting some favourites. Encourage them to think about who their audience will be at home and to find a suitable poem for that family member. When each child has chosen a favourite poem, either give them time to copy it out or photocopy it so that they have it to take home. Explain to children that they are to take their poems home and share with a family member and see what their reaction is.

> 3. Make sure you leave time the following day for the children to describe their experience of reading a poem to a family member. If you have had positive responses from parents and they are prepared to come in and share their favourite poems with the class, then this would be a good opportunity to do this.

Variations

- If parents are keen to participate, they could write down their responses to the poems they have heard; these could be posted in a 'response to poetry' box within the classroom. At the end of the week, the box could be opened and the responses shared. This would undoubtedly lead to a discussion relating to personal preferences and differences of opinion, which is a vital component of a primary classroom.

Cross-curricular links

PSHE – recognising what people like and dislike and respecting different opinions.

Spreading the word

Enthusiasm and excitement in schools are infectious. This activity is designed to ensure that a love of poetry spreads through your school like a disease.

Suitable for

KS1
KS2

Aims

- To promote a love of poetry.

Resources

- Poetry books and anthologies
- Poetry websites (see Appendix 6)

What to do

1. This activity is probably best to engage with when you are about half way through the school year. By this time you will have shared hundreds of poems with the children and they will be beginning to identify favourite poems and poets.
2. As a class, discuss favourite poems and poets. Read some poems aloud and refamiliarise the children with the work of different poets.
3. Explain to the children that they are going to engage in a range of activities that are all linked with promoting a love of poetry throughout the school. There will be different areas within the classroom, and the children can choose which area they would like to join according to the activity they would like to be involved in. The areas could include the following:

   - **Poetry scribing** – children copy out their favourite poems and illustrate them.

- **Making displays** – these could be made for corridors, the school hall, the head teacher's office, the entrance foyer etc.
- **Creating lists** – favourite poems and poets (this could be linked with Internet research if you have access to computers in the room).
- **Making posters** – promote poems and poets through posters, which could be displayed around the school.
- **Preparing an assembly** – one group of children could prepare a short presentation to share with the school, describing the project.

4. If you have time, these areas could remain in place all day and children could move from one to another as appropriate.
5. By the end of this activity, you should have a wealth of resources linked to poetry that can be shared with the school.

Variations

- The whole school could be involved with this project. Instead of having all the different activities in one class, teachers could decide in advance which activity their class will undertake; at the end of the day, a whole school assembly could be used to share the work produced from all classes.

Cross-curricular links

Art – there are plenty of opportunities to link art with this activity.

Playing the prediction game

A useful strategy to make children aware of when they are learning to read is that of prediction – predicting what word is likely to come next. Rhyming poetry is particularly useful to support this.

Suitable for

KS1

Aims

- To use prediction as a reading strategy.

Resources

- You can use any of your favourite rhyming poems but here are two suggestions:
  - 'Little Red Riding Hood and the Wolf' by Roald Dahl: www.poetryarchive.org/childrensarchive/singlePoem.do?poemId=7428
  - 'My Cat Goes Flying Through The Air' by Kenn Nesbitt: www.poetry4kids.com/poem-505.html

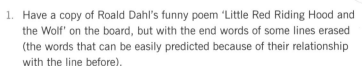

What to do

1. Have a copy of Roald Dahl's funny poem 'Little Red Riding Hood and the Wolf' on the board, but with the end words of some lines erased (the words that can be easily predicted because of their relationship with the line before).
2. Explain to the children that you are going to read them a funny poem about Little Red Riding Hood but it will also be a game because you are going to stop at certain points and they have to guess the missing word. Ask them to raise their hand if they think they can predict the missing word.

3. As you go through the poem, record on the board the children's suggestions for the missing words, but do not tell them if they are right or wrong. After this first reading, play them the recording of Dahl reading the poem (see the website above) and compare the correct version with the ideas the children offered. It is likely that most of their predictions will be correct and you can then discuss how it was that they could do this – rhyme, context, meaning etc.

4. Explain to the children that if they get stuck on a word, it can sometimes help to predict what might come next, as they have just experienced. Repeat the game with another poem – you could use Kenn Nesbitt's poem 'My Cat Goes Flying Through the Air' (see the website above) and again listen to the poet reciting the poem to check the children's predictions.

Variations

- Pair the children up. Instead of raising their hand when they want to make a prediction, ask them to work together to write the word on a mini whiteboard. By the end they will have a list of words that they can check as the poem is read out with the missing words in place.

Cross-curricular links

PSHE – developing the confidence to try different strategies. Being prepared to have a go and not worrying that you might make mistakes along the way.

Patterns in poetry

When children are learning to read, it helps if they can begin to spot certain patterns that occur. Rhyming poems often follow a very regular pattern and are therefore a useful tool to use.

Suitable for

KS1

Aims

- To identify word patterns in poems.

Resources

- 'The Day I Got My Finger Stuck Up My Nose' by Brian Patten: www.poemhunter.com/poem/the-day-i-got-my-finger-stuck-up-my-nose/
- 'Please Mrs Butler' by Allan Ahlberg: www.poemhunter.com/poem/please-mrs-butler/

What to do

1. Explain to the children that you are going to read them a poem and they need to think about any patterns in the poem. For example, is there something that happens in every verse? Have a copy of the poem on the board so that they can see the visual patterns as well as hearing the words.
2. Read 'The Day I Got My Finger Stuck Up My Nose' by Brian Patten (you may want to have a discussion about the poet's name!). Did you spot any patterns? They might suggest the repetition of four lines in each verse; the rhyming pattern of a b c b; repetition of the words 'said' and 'head'; the fact that there is only one rhyming sound throughout the poem.

3. Discuss with the children how this might help us with our reading – if a poem follows a set pattern, it makes it easy to predict what some of the words might be.
4. Repeat the activity with 'Please Mrs Butler' by Allan Ahlberg. This time the children could work in pairs to come up with two patterns that they can spot in the poem. Feed back to the class.

Variations

- Spotting patterns can also help children with their spelling. They can begin to identify where some words sound the same and are spelt with the same pattern of words, e.g. 'vest' and 'best' in 'Please Mrs Butler', and also where some words sound the same but are spelt differently, e.g. 'said' and 'head' in 'The Day I Got My Finger Stuck Up My Nose'.

Cross-curricular links

Maths, art and music – patterns are an important element of these three subjects. Once you have brought this to the attention of young children, they will soon be spotting patterns everywhere. It could be a subject for topic work.

Fun with phonics

There are a wealth of phonic activities in numerous publications and online resources. I think that one of the best ways to teach different sounds is through poems, where the sounds crop up time and time again and are contextualised in 'real' writing.

Suitable for

KS1

Aims

- To link sound and letter patterns, exploring rhyme, alliteration and other sound patterns.

Resources

- Examples of rhyming poems and rhyming picture books (Julia Donaldson's picture books are very useful and great fun to read)
- www.bbc.co.uk/schools/wordsandpictures/longvow/poems/fpoem.shtml – this website has activities which combine poems, animation and audio effects
- www.poetry4kids.com/modules.php?name=Rhymes&op=search – this website has an online rhyming dictionary, which is very useful for spotting links between sounds and letters
- 'My Friend Elsie' by Michael Rosen: www.poetryarchive.org/childrensarchive/singlePoem.do?poemId=448

What to do

1. Depending on the sound you wish to explore with the children, choose some poems that are appropriate. 'My friend Elsie' by Michael Rosen explores a range of sounds, including 'ee' and 'oo'. It is important to build up a bank of these poems, which can help you

contextualise letters and sounds. The BBC website above has some useful poems that are linked with animation and sound; they are interactive, so the children can get really involved.

2. Once you have read the poem, ask the children to identify any sounds that occur more than once. Give them an example first, e.g. if you are using Rosen's poem, you might point out 'red' and 'bed' as both having the 'e' sound. Reread the poem, stopping every time someone spots some recurring sounds.

3. Choose one sound in particular and ask the children if they know of any other words that have the same sound. List these on the board. Go to the poetry4kids website, which has a rhyming dictionary. Type in the word 'bed' (for example) and then click on 'most common words first'; the website will produce a list of words with the same sound. You could compare this with the list made by the children and add any words that they did not mention. These word lists could be displayed/stuck into the children's books as a resource to support the children with their reading and writing.

Variations

- Give the children some poetry books to look through and ask them to find any examples of a particular sound being used in a poem. These poems can then be used to illustrate the sound. If this is done as a regular activity, the children can make books of poems relating to different sounds.

Rhythm and rhyme

Poems with a very regular beat and a predictable rhyme scheme can help children build their confidence with reading. They begin to recognise and absorb the cadences used by specific poets and thus develop their own fluency.

Suitable for

KS1

Aims

- To use rhythm and rhyme to help develop fluency.

Resources

- Poems with very predictable rhythms and rhymes, such as:
  - 'A Kangaroo' by Julie Holder: http://heatheranne.freeservers.com/childrens/akangaro.htm
  - 'Betty at the Party' (anonymous): http://heatheranne.freeservers.com/childrens/BettyAtTheParty.htm

What to do

1. Read 'A Kangaroo' by Julie Holder, with the words up on the board for the children to see. Read the poem again, but this time hide the words and ask the children to see if they can say the last word of each verse. How did you know what the word would be?
2. Read the poem again, but this time as you read, clap on every second and fourth word in each line, so that each verse has eight beats. This will emphasise the rhythm of the poem (try to read it in a very rhythmic way). Read the poem again, asking a volunteer to clap for each verse, while the other children read with you.

3. Now ask for three volunteers, one to read each verse; ask another three volunteers to clap the rhythm for each verse. The rest of the class join in with the last word of each verse.

4. By this time, most of the children will probably know the whole poem off by heart. Because of this, they should be able to recite with you, one more time, fluently and maintaining an appropriate rhythm.

5. Repeat the activity with the poem 'Betty at the Party'. In this poem there is plenty of speech, so you could get children to take different parts.

Variations

- With the poem 'Betty at the Party', the children could put together a role play to go with the poem; this would promote a deeper appreciation of the rhythms and cadences of this poem.

Looking for meaning

Some poems are quite ambiguous and the reader needs to interpret them in their own way. This can be challenging for young children, but this activity should get them started.

Suitable for

KS1

Aims

- To focus on meaning derived from the text as a whole.

Resources

- 'The Land of Story Books' by Robert Louis Stevenson: www.lone-star.net/mall/literature/rls/LandofStorybooks.htm
- The picture book *Where the Wild Things Are* by Maurice Sendak

What to do

1. Read 'The Land of Story Books' by Robert Louis Stevenson. What do you think this poem is about? Who is the writer of the poem?
2. Make sure all the children can see a copy of the poem and reread it to them. Are there any words they do not understand? You may need to discuss the 'lamp' being lit and the child's 'nurse'. Where does the child go? Does he really go to these places – to hills, rivers, woods, meeting lions and Indians? What clues are there that these adventures are all part of his imagination? Have you ever pretended that you are in a jungle or forest or desert or on a wild sea? Discuss with the person next to you the wildest adventure you have had, within your own house. What do you think he means when he goes to bed 'with backward looks'?

3. Does this poem remind you of anything else you have read? It is very similar to *Where the Wild Things Are* by Maurice Sendak. Has anyone seen the film?
4. Read the Sendak picture book to the class and discuss the similarities with the Stevenson poem.

Variations

- Share with the children 'Pirate Story' and 'Escape at Bedtime', also by Stevenson, and discuss the similarities.

Syllables or silly bulls?

Having an understanding of syllables can be a great help when children are developing as readers and writers. Poetic structure is often based on a certain number of syllables, and so poems make a good context for discussion.

Suitable for

KS2

Aims

- To recognise syllables within poems and to use this knowledge to develop reading and spelling strategies.

Resources

- Examples of haikus
- Poems with rhyming couplets
- 'Little Red Riding Hood and the Wolf' by Roald Dahl: www.poetryarchive.org/childrensarchive/singlePoem.do?poemId=7428

What to do

1. What is a syllable? How many syllables are in your first name? How many syllables are in 'elephant'? How might an understanding of syllables help us with reading and spelling? Give the children some time to discuss these questions.
2. Read some poems that are written in rhyming couplets. Discuss rhyming couplets – how they often have the same number of syllables in each line and follow a very regular pattern. Read 'Little Red Riding Hood and the Wolf' by Roald Dahl – this has a very regular rhythm and rhyme, and each line has eight syllables. Reread a few lines, with the children clapping the syllables.

3. Set a task – write two lines on any subject, to make a rhyming couplet that has the same amount of syllables in each line. Model an example, e.g.

   I sat at home, so very bored
   My friend had left and gone abroad.

   You could mention here, how 'bored' and 'abroad' sound the same but are spelt differently.

4. Create a whole class rhyming couplet as a shared writing exercise so that the children begin to get the idea of rhyming and syllables.

5. Working in pairs, ask the children to have a go at the task and then share their couplets with the class.

Variations

- It would be great fun as a class to make up a long poem in the same style as Roald Dahl's 'Little Red Riding Hood and the Wolf', focusing on rhyme and syllables. This could then be turned into a performance poem.

Cross-curricular links

Literacy – spelling. Developing strategies to help with spelling unknown words.

Paying attention to punctuation

Heeding punctuation is an important aspect of developing fluency in reading, whether reading aloud or silent reading. If punctuation is ignored, the meaning of a text can be compromised. Poems are good places to look for unusual punctuation.

Suitable for

KS2

Aims

- To read with fluency, accuracy and understanding.

Resources

- 'The Runaway' by Robert Frost: www.internal.org/Robert_Frost/The_Runaway

What to do

1. Give each child a copy of 'The Runaway' by Robert Frost or have it enlarged on the board. Read the poem to the children, really focusing on the punctuation – pausing where appropriate, raising your voice for the questions, using a different voice for the speech etc.
2. Give the children time to discuss the poem and ask any questions. Give them some background information about Robert Frost, who lived in Vermont on a farm, and Morgan horses, which are an American breed, so that they are able to contextualise the poem.
3. How important is punctuation when reading poems or any other text? What does punctuation do? Make a list of punctuation 'jobs' on the board, e.g. makes you pause, tells you how to read a particular word/line, ensures that the reader gets the message that the writer wishes to pass on etc.

4. Ask the children to highlight all the punctuation in the poem, either on their sheets or on the board. Discuss the different punctuation. Draw the children's attention to the fact that sometimes, although you move on to a new line, your reading needs to be continuous, e.g. in line 4, you need to read without pausing from 'He dipped his head' through to the full stop in the middle of line 5. Why does the poet put full stops in the middle of lines? In this way he can capture the mood and tone – the nervousness and energy of the young horse.

5. Reread the poem, asking the children to pay particular attention to how the punctuation affects the reading. If there is time, volunteers can read parts of the poem aloud.

Informed guesses

> Whatever age you are, however experienced you are as a reader, you will always come across words that you have not heard before and for which you do not have a meaning. One of the first strategies in these instances is to make informed guesses, using the context.

Suitable for

KS2

Aims

- To use contexts to help with making meaning of unfamiliar vocabulary.

Resources

- 'Tartary' by Walter de la Mare: www.poemhunter.com/poem/tartary/

What to do

1. Explain to the children that you are going to read them a poem by a famous poet and that there might be words within the poem that they have not heard before. Tell them not to worry, but just to enjoy the sound and rhythms of the poem.
2. Read 'Tartary' by Walter de la Mare and then discuss their opinions and ideas.
3. Ask the children to get into pairs. Give each pair a copy of the poem and ask them to work together to highlight any words where they are not sure of the meaning. When they have done this, take three of the words and have a go at guessing the meaning and make a note on a mini whiteboard.
4. Reread the poem and ask the children to raise their hand if you come to a word that they are unsure of. The first word might be

'flaunt' in line 5. Does anyone know what this might mean? Could you have a guess? What would your guess be based upon? You might consider characteristics of a peacock – they tend to strut around showing off their feathers. So what might 'flaunt' mean? Try to use the context to help you with understanding.

5. Continue through the poem, encouraging the children to make informed guesses when they are unsure of meanings.

Variations

- If the children are confident 'guessers', they could work through the poem; when they get to a word where they are unsure of the meaning, they could have a guess and replace the word with a word(s) that might mean the same. For example, for 'flaunt', they might put 'show off'. This will really extend their knowledge and understanding of vocabulary.

Making miracles

This activity uses the wonderful poem 'Miracles' by Walt Whitman. Children can immerse themselves in the poet's thoughts and think about what is miraculous to them.

Suitable for

KS2

Aims

- To consider the effects of particular poetic devices.
- To share views on a poem.

Resources

- 'Miracles' by Walt Whitman (see Appendix 1p)

What to do

1. What do you think the word 'miracle' means? What is a miracle? Ask someone to look up the dictionary definition and write it on the board.
2. Read 'Miracles' by Walt Whitman. What does the poet consider to be miraculous? Do these not seem very simple things? Why do you think he considers these to be miracles? (There are no 'right' answers here – the questions should merely promote discussion.)
3. Give the children five minutes to work in their groups to come up with a question they might ask the poet if he were still alive. Share the questions. One of the questions I would like to ask him is why he uses the word 'or' at the beginning of ten consecutive lines. What effect does this have? What other word does he use a great deal?
4. Ask a volunteer to reread the poem. Ask the class: Do you like the poem? Discuss with a partner why you like/dislike the poem.
5. What, to you, are miracles in life?

Variations

- The children could look more carefully at the language used in this poem. Doing this, they could situate it within a context (Manhattan?) and a time/place (use of imperial measurements). They might then want to go on to find out more about this poet.

Cross-curricular links

Religious education – the children may associate miracles with stories in the Bible, so a comparison could be made between biblical miracles and Whitman's miracles.

Totally terrific titles

The titles of poems tend to give away what the poem will be about. By removing the title and encouraging children to invent their own, you are assessing their understanding of the poem.

Suitable for

KS2

Aims

- To co-construct knowledge and understanding.

Resources

- 'The Eagle' by Alfred, Lord Tennyson: www.poemhunter.com/poem/the-eagle/
- 'Seal' by William Jay Smith: http://beingintotalcontrolhoney.blogspot.com/ 2007/11/seal-by-william-jay-smith.html – don't let the children see the picture that goes with this poem because it will give the game away

What to do

1. Explain to the children that you are going to read them a poem, but you are not going to give them the title of the poem. Working in groups as 'poet detectives', they are going to look for clues from the words of the poem and have a go at guessing the title.
2. Read 'The Eagle' by Alfred, Lord Tennyson. Give each group a copy of the poem (without the title). Encourage them to look at specific language used, using dictionaries if necessary to check the meaning of words.
3. Ask each group to write a title on their mini whiteboard. Go around the class, listing possible titles on the board and asking each group how they came to decide on a title. What were the key words?

4. Tell the children the title of the poem and reread it, asking the children to look for relevant clues.
5. Repeat the activity with 'Seal' by William Jay Smith.

Variations

- The children can have great fun with this, making up their own poems, not telling anyone the title and then testing their peers.

Cross-curricular links

Science – the children could make up a short poem about a scientific object/concept, without mentioning it by name in the poem but leaving clues throughout. They could then test their peers.

Chapter 10
Ideas to promote writing

Introduction

This chapter has a slightly different format from the others: it is divided into three sections to reflect what I consider to be the three main aspects of writing that need to be considered by both teachers and learners. The first of these is the use of form. Both novice and experienced writers can gain a great deal from using the writing of others as a model for their own compositions. This might mean that they follow the structure or setting of a short story, the plot and characterisation of a novel, or (more relevant to this book) the form/style/tone/patterns of an existing poem. In this way they develop their knowledge and understanding of a particular form and gain confidence, leading ultimately to a more independent approach to writing reflecting their own unique ideas and style. Using other people's forms can, however, be quite prescriptive, so I have also included activities that reflect a greater degree of freedom, where children are encouraged to be creative and there is less emphasis on following a particular route. Finally, I felt it was important to consider presentation and publication, as these are vital components of writing. Children need to feel proud of the writing they have produced and be encouraged to consider both audience and purpose.

The first section has six activities and is based on structured writing tasks that use existing poems as scaffolds for children's own poetry writing. The next section also has six activities, but they are designed to give the children more freedom, allowing them to decide what they want to write about and the poetic form they wish to use to represent their ideas. The final section has three ideas and these are linked with presentation and publication.

Using existing poems or poetic forms as scaffolds for writing

Writing on a theme

I am sure that you use themes within your classroom, around which speaking and listening, reading and writing can be planned. Common themes are the weather, the seaside, zoos etc. This activity shows how poetry can be linked in with different themes.

Suitable for

KS1

Aims

- To write poetry linked to a theme.

Resources

- Poetry linked to themes
- www.earlyliterature.ecsd.net/resources1.htm

What to do

1. Investigate the website above. This is a fantastic site, with 33 different themes to choose from. When you have chosen a theme, you can find poems, rhymes, raps, chants etc. that match the theme. The themes include dinosaurs, alphabet, holidays, friendship, bugs and feelings.
2. Find a theme that fits into something you are working on with your class. Spend some time sharing the literature that you find on the site – singing the songs, playing the games etc.

3. Choose a particular poem or song with a very familiar structure –
    for example, under the 'Sea Life' section, there is a song entitled
    'A Fishing We Will Go'; the site suggests that it is sung to the tune of
    'A Hunting We Will Go'. Sing this a few times and then suggest to the
    children that, as a class, you construct your own version to go with
    the same tune.

4. Ask the children to discuss in pairs the activity with which they would
    like to replace fishing and model your own version. You could use the
    following as a model if you wished:

    A skipping we will go, a skipping we will go
    We'll have some fun, skipping in the sun
    A skipping we will go.
    A skipping we will go, a skipping we will go
    Girls and boys, come and enjoy!
    A skipping we will go.

    By Virginia Bower

5. Ask the children to share their ideas and engage the children in
    shared writing, scribing their ideas into the familiar chosen format.
    You can then sing your new song.

Variations

- If the children seem confident once you have modelled your version, they
  could work in pairs or independently to produce their own songs based
  around the same format.

Cross-curricular links

Music – responding to a range of musical and non-musical starting points.

A poem to apologise

This activity provides pupils with a strong scaffold for their own poem writing and was very successful each time I used it with my class. Every child, whatever their ability, was able to produce a poem.

Suitable for

KS2

Aims

- To write a poem in the style of a particular poet.

Resources

- 'this is just to say' by William Carlos Williams: http://en.wikipedia.org/wiki/This_Is_Just_To_Say#Text_of_the_poem

What to do

1. Read the poem 'this is just to say' by William Carlos Williams. What do you notice about the poem (absence of punctuation, capital letters, unusual layout etc.)? Why do you think the poet writes in this way? Do you like it?

2. What is the poem about? Ask the children to discuss in groups any times in their lives where they have had to be forgiven for something they have done. Share any experiences with the whole class.

3. Show the class an example of a poem that you have written in the same style – here is one I used with my class:

   this is just to say
   i have not completed
   my homework
   which was due in

> *today*
> *forgive me*
> *the sun was so warm*
> *and my new bike*
> *so tempting*
>
> By Virginia Bower
>
> 4. Discuss the format and how the original poem can be used as a template (if they wish to do so). It is important to emphasise that this format does not have to be strictly adhered to – it can be used merely as a guide – otherwise the children can become frustrated with not being able to find the 'correct' word or line length.
> 5. Children can then work in pairs or individually to produce their own poems in the style of Williams. These poems make an excellent display.

Variations

- Other poems can be used in the same way. It is good to choose poems with strong, clear structures or that have something unusual about them that the children will enjoy imitating. 'The Magic Box' by Kit Wright is another useful poem to use in the same way.

Cross-curricular links

PSHE – owning up to misdeeds; being forgiven.

Alternative versions

This activity uses an existing poem as a scaffold for children's poetry writing. However, it offers a little less support than the previous activity (A poem to apologise) and is therefore more challenging. Make sure that the children are fairly confident with the idea of writing poetry and have already engaged in a range of poetry writing activities before attempting this.

Suitable for

KS2

Aims

- To write an alternative version of an existing poem.

Resources

- A variety of poems with strong structures:
  - ''Twas the Night Before Christmas' by Clement C Moore: www.carols.org. uk/twas_the_night_before_christmas.htm
  - 'The Magic Box' by Kit Wright: http://mayfield.ealing.lgfl.digitalbrain.com/ lgfl/leas/ealing/schools/mayfield/web/Communities/Year5/resources/main/ Literacy/magic_box/

What to do

1. Explain to the children that they are going to write an alternative version of an existing poem.
2. Read one of the poems you have chosen (I am going to base this example on ''Twas the Night Before Christmas' but you can use any poem with a strong structure). What do the children notice about the poem? It has a regular rhythm and rhyme; it tells a story; it has clear verses where the line length and basic structure remains the same etc.

3. Model the beginning of an alternative version, e.g.

'Twas the day after Christmas,
And all through the town
Children were playing,
As snow fluttered down;

Brand new sledges
All on display,
Shrieks of excitement,
On this Boxing Day.
        By Virginia Bower

4. Discuss how the original features have been retained, while the focus has changed. As a class, write a third verse for this alternative version.

5. If the children seem confident, ask them to work in pairs or individually to produce another verse. In this way, a class poem can be produced.

Variations

- Instead of writing a whole new poem, the children could write an extra verse for an existing poem, focusing on keeping the structure and rhythm while taking the poem in another direction.

Cross-curricular links

Geography – you could select poems about places around the world and the children could use the poems' structures, while choosing an alternative location as the subject matter.

It's a jungle out there!

Children need to be exposed to clever use of poetic devices such as personification. This activity is based on the poem 'City Jungle' by Pie Corbett, where the use of language is superb.

Suitable for

KS2

Aims

- To introduce children to personification and how it can be used effectively.

Resources

- 'City Jungle' by Pie Corbett – if you put this into an Internet search engine, a resource sheet will be on the list of sites, with the full version of the poem.

What to do

1. Read the poem 'City Jungle' to the children. Ask them to work in pairs to note down all the references that seem more appropriate to animals than to city life. Collect ideas and record on the board.
2. The poet is using personification (where human qualities are given to inanimate objects) to create a particular effect. What effect is this? What images do his words place in your mind? Ask the children to choose their favourite line and to discuss with their group why they have chosen this line.
3. Explain to the children that they are going to work in groups to come up with some ideas of how we might personify classroom objects, e.g. 'the door yawned open', 'the chair legs screamed with horror as the teacher sat down'. Give them some time to work on this and then gather in their ideas.

4. Scribe all the groups' ideas on the board and then work together (shared writing) to produce a class poem, focusing on effective use of personification. This poem could form part of a poetry display; the children could create some art work to go with their writing.

Variations

- This poem lends itself beautifully to drama. The children could act out the poem as it is read, taking on the characteristics described. This would reinforce the idea of personification and the fact that it is based on human characteristics.

Cross-curricular links

Music – this would be a great poem to put to music, even if the children were only using body percussion.

Art – the images created by this poem could be used as a base for children's art work.

Poetry maps

One of the best ways by which to promote poetry writing is to tap into the children's life outside school and encourage them to use their memories and personal experiences as inspiration for their poems. This activity encourages children to 'map' an experience and use this as a plan for their poems.

Suitable for

KS1
KS2

Aims

- To use a 'poetry map' to plan and write a poem based on personal experience.

Resources

- Poems about personal experiences:
  - 'Picnic' by Judith Nicholls: www.poetryarchive.org/childrensarchive/ singlePoem.do?poemId=395
  - 'Dad and the Cat and the Tree' by Kit Wright (from the anthology 'Rabbiting On')
  - 'Father and Child' by Allan Ahlberg

What to do

1. Read the children a selection of poems about personal experiences. Choose one poem in particular and reread it, asking the children to pinpoint key moments in the poem. Record these on a poetry 'map', e.g. if the poem is about a trip to the beach, you could record the phrases 'home', 'car', 'arguing', 'arrive at beach', 'sand in sandwiches', 'cold sea', 'building castles', 'rain storm', 'sleepy journey home'. These can be recorded in words or pictures.

2. In pairs, ask the children to discuss a trip they have taken somewhere, thinking about the sequence of events. Share some examples with the class.

3. Ask the children to create their own 'maps' to describe a journey/ experience/trip.

4. Ask the children to tell the story of their experience, using their map, to a talk partner. In this way they are verbalising what will eventually be written down as a poem.

5. Use one of the maps created by a child as an example and model how it might be turned into a poem, e.g.

I woke up early
Sun streaming in the window
A perfect day
For the beach!

Bags packed
Sandwiches made
Suncream on
Can't wait – let's go!

    By Virginia Bower

6. Ask the children to use their poetry maps to write their own poems.

Variations

- To focus the children's ideas and to enable them to draw on a wide range of vocabulary, you might suggest they all write on a theme, e.g. a trip to the beach or a day out shopping (making sure, of course, that all the children in the class have had a relevant experience).

Cross-curricular links

Depending on the theme chosen for the poems, you could link to geography (trips to different places), science (nature, animals, seasons) and maths (coordinates).

Rhyming madness

If you are not careful when teaching poetry, the children can become obsessed with making everything rhyme. This can lead to poems that make little sense and are rather uninspiring. However, at times it is great to allow children to indulge in the fun of rhymes – and this activity promotes just that.

Suitable for

KS1
KS2

Aims

- To promote the effective use of rhyme in poems.

Resources

- A wide selection of rhyming poems. Here are a few examples you could access online:
  - 'On the way to school' by Charles Ghigna: www.blackcatpoems.com/g/on_the_way_to_school.html
  - 'Sandra Slater' by John Foster (can be found in the anthology *Read Me and Laugh* by Gaby Morgan)
  - 'Little Red Riding Hood and the Wolf' by Roald Dahl: www.poetryarchive.org/childrensarchive/singlePoem.do?poemId=7428

What to do

1. Read to the class a selection of poems that have rhyming patterns. Ask them to identify rhyming words and to recognise when the spelling is different, e.g. in 'On the Way to School' there are words such as 'do', 'due', 'hue' and 'Peekaboo'. It is important that the children realise that they may come across many words that rhyme but that do not look the same when written down.

2. Write a word on the board, e.g. 'shake'. Ask the children to work in groups to come up with as many words as possible that rhyme with shake. Give them five minutes to work on this and then ask each group to feed back their words while you make a list on the board. Explain to the children that if they wish to write rhyming poems, they need to have a large bank of words to draw on.

3. Repeat the task with other words so that you end up with banks of rhyming words (the children could do this as a task at home, collecting rhyming words and bringing them back to school to add to the lists).

4. Choose one of the lists and try to link some of the words with a mini story, e.g. if you had 'shake', 'make', 'take', 'wake' and 'break' you could have a story about waking up in the morning and wanting to make a milkshake – but as you take the glass out of the cupboard, it breaks. Go back to the poems that were shared at the beginning of the lesson and identify whether they tell stories and how the rhymes are used.

5. If there is time, the children could write their own poems using the word banks, or the whole class could create a joint poem.

Variations

● Introduce a theme a week, e.g. weather, and encourage the children to create class word banks linked with the theme that can be added to at any point and used for poetry writing and story writing.

Cross-curricular links

Spelling – although this is still within the topic of literacy, and therefore not strictly cross-curricular, it is too good an opportunity to miss. To a certain extent, the children will be absorbing the different spelling patterns as you discuss the rhymes. However, you can use the poems to teach specific spelling rules; because they are contextualised within poems, the children will be more likely to remember them.

Less structured activities, promoting independence and creativity

Objects of inspiration

This activity gives the children a starting point for their writing but then leaves them free to choose the direction in which their poem will go. It might be better to save this activity until they have had the opportunity to explore and enjoy many poems.

Suitable for

KS1
KS2

Aims

- To use an object as the inspiration for poetry writing.

Resources

- A range of different objects

What to do

1. Have a box of objects that you have gathered from home/holidays/the school environment, e.g. shells, old books, jewellery, old coins. Do not let the children see what is inside the box. Ask one member of each group to come up, put their hand in the box and take out an object and return to their table.

2. Give the children time to discuss the object and pose questions about it. Give them the opportunity to touch, smell and study the object. After five minutes, each group passes their object to another group and you repeat the discussion time. This can be repeated until everyone has had the chance to see all the objects.

3. Remind the children of all the different poems they have encountered in their school and home life – those that rhyme and those that do not; short, funny verses; long narratives; poems that play on words; list poems etc.

4. Tell them that they are free to write using any form they wish. They can use the objects they have been studying as the inspiration for their poems, or they can choose an object of their own.

5. Give them time to create their own poems (taking them home to finish if they wish to) and arrange to have a time in which they can share their creations with the class if they wish to.

Variations

- The object could be replaced by music – playing different pieces of music to the children, or allowing them to bring in their own favourite tunes. Music could then be the inspiration for their poetry writing.

Cross-curricular links

Science – inevitably when children are describing objects they are likely to discuss their properties, such as smooth, shiny and metallic; these words can be linked with science topics.

Music – see the idea in Variations above.

Collaborative creations

With this activity, children are free to explore their own ideas, but in a collaborative way. It is a really fun way to encourage children who might lack confidence with poetry writing.

Suitable for

KS1
KS2

Aims

- To create poems, building on the ideas of others.

Resources

- Large pieces of lined/plain paper. If you have coloured paper/gel or coloured pens, this can make a big difference to the children's motivation to write

What to do

1. Tell the children that everyone is going to write the title and first two lines of a poem, about anything they like. Model an example, e.g.

   First day at school
   I stand in the playground
   All alone

2. Once they have written the title and first two lines, they leave their paper on their desk and move around the room, looking at the writing of their peers. When they find a title and first two lines that appeal to them, they then have to add another two lines to the existing

writing. For example, if they like the title and two lines modelled above, they could continue on this theme:

First day at school
I stand in the playground
All alone
My heart is pounding
My legs are weak.

3. This continues until they have added to several poems. If they feel they can write the concluding two lines for someone, then they may do this. If not, after several moves around the room, the children return to their original poem, read it through and finish it.
4. Discuss the ideas that have been contributed. Do the children like the way their poem has evolved? If there is time, the children could read their poems aloud, and other children who have contributed to that particular poem could comment on the finished product.

Variations

- This can be made into a quick, funny game. Give the children a theme, e.g. chocolate. They have to write one line of a poem and then fold the paper over, so that the next person cannot see what they have written. The paper is passed on to the person sitting next to them and that person adds another line relating to chocolate. Once the papers have been around the whole group and they return to the original owner, the poems can be read – this usually causes great amusement!

Cross-curricular links

PSHE – working and playing collaboratively and cooperatively.

My life

Sometimes children say that they can't think of anything to write about. This activity gives them the opportunity to write about any aspect of their lives – so no excuses for lack of ideas!

Suitable for

KS1
KS2

Aims

- To explore experience through poetry.

Resources

- Michael Rosen has written many poems based on experiences within his own life. His official website has some great poems you can use, e.g. 'Attack', 'Pelicans' and 'A Dangerous Raisin': www.michaelrosen.co.uk/poems.html

What to do

1. Read some of the poems by Michael Rosen based upon experiences within his own life. Discuss the incidents that might have provoked these poems.
2. In pairs, ask the children to take turns to describe a funny/scary/weird/ sad incident in their own lives.
3. Explain to the children that they are going to create their own poems based upon an experience/incident in their own lives. This could be a simple description of an ordinary day, from getting up in the morning to going to bed at night, or it could focus on a small/large experience that affected them in some way.
4. You could model an example, but this activity is concerned with the children developing their own creative writing and giving them freedom. Sometimes, providing models can restrict their own imaginations. This will depend on your class – you know them best!

Variations

- Although it is a little more restrictive, you could encourage the children to all write poems on the same experience, e.g. a school trip, sports day or parents' evening. This allows them to be creative but gives them a starting point. It is fun to then compare the poems on one subject.

Cross-curricular links

PSHE – encouraging the children to think about their own lives and learn from their experiences.

Music as a starting point

This section of the chapter is all about promoting independence and creativity. However, sometimes providing a starting point of some sort can inspire and motivate; in this activity, music is the key.

Suitable for

KS1
KS2

Aims

● To use music as a starting point for poetry writing.

Resources

● Popular classical music – preferably a range of examples, including powerful and dramatic, quiet and dreamy, and exciting and energising.

What to do

1. Explain to the children that they are going to write poems on whatever they like, but that you are going to play them some music to use as a starting point if they wish to.
2. Play a range of musical pieces and give the children a chance to talk about each one after it is played. If they want to, they could jot down any ideas that occur to them as they listen. Try not to lead the conversation with your own ideas and opinions – let them verbalise their thoughts and feelings without your influence. This is important if they are to be allowed the freedom to go off in whatever direction they choose. Younger children may find this very difficult, as they may be used to quite a bit of direction.

3. The children may wish to listen to the pieces again, or just their favourites. If you have the facilities for the children to listen on headphones or in other areas of the school, then they may want to get together in groups or go off alone to listen to the music.
4. When they are ready, they can begin to turn their thoughts about the music they have listened to into a poem.

Variations

* You might want to use only one piece of music that you think would inspire the children to write. They could then all produce poems inspired by this piece and compare their compositions. Interpretation of music inevitably differs from person to person, so you should get some great variety.

Cross-curricular links

Music – obviously!
PSHE – recognising how music can change our moods and feelings.

Beyond the classroom walls

I believe that every opportunity should be taken to get the children out of the classroom and into the outside environment. Inspiration for poetry writing is more likely to come from what children might consider a change from the norm.

Suitable for

KS1
KS2

Aims

* To use the outside environment as a stimulus for poetry writing.

Resources

* An outside environment. Some of us are luckier than others and have playing fields, outside play areas, nearby parks etc. However, if you do not have these facilities, perhaps it would be possible to plan in the time to walk to a local park. If not, you can always use the playground – there should still be plenty for the children to see and hear

What to do

1. Take the children to whatever outside environment you have access to. Explain that they are going to use the outside environment as a stimulus for writing a poem. They need to think about the sights, sounds and sensations they are exposed to that are different from being in the classroom.
2. Leave the children to explore (within reason!) and collect ideas.
3. If the environment and weather are suitable, the children could work on clipboards and begin writing their poems while still outside. If this is not possible, then they can make notes and do the writing back inside the classroom.

4. Give the children time to write their poems and then compare with others. It will be interesting to see how they differ, how some children may have focused more on the things they see and others on what they have heard.

Variations

- The children could collect an object from the outside environment and write a poem about this object, such as a leaf, pebble or empty crisp packet.

Cross-curricular links

Science – senses, the natural world, forces etc.
Art – the children may wish to illustrate their poems, basing their illustrations on their outside experience.

Tantalising titles

I was not sure whether to put this activity in the 'freedom and creativity' section, because you, as the teacher, will have a certain amount of control here. However, I still think this idea promotes independent writing, so here it is.

Suitable for

KS1
KS2

Aims

● To choose form and content to suit a particular purpose.

Resources

● A list of possible poem titles (see some examples below)
● Interesting paper/pencils to inspire the children to write

What to do

1. Give the children a list of poem titles, e.g.

   Along Came a Spider
   The Day I Met Superman
   Autumn
   My Pet Alligator
   Aches and Pains
   Favourite Places

2. Explain to the children that they need to choose one of these titles upon which to base their poem. Give them a few tips, e.g. if they like to write descriptive poems using adjectives and similes, then they might choose a poem about autumn. If they want to write a funny poem or use a particular form, e.g. a limerick, then they may want to choose a title about a pet alligator.

3. Discuss how we all write differently and have different interests, and that this is important when choosing what we want to write about.
4. If the children seem uninspired by your list of titles (and I am sure they will tell you!), let them add some titles to the list.
5. Give the children time to write their poems and then group them according to the title they have chosen. They can then share their poems with those children who have written about the same subject and compare their ideas.

Variations

- Give the whole class one title and ask all the children to write a poem based on this title. Share and compare ideas.

Cross-curricular links

The titles could reflect topics you have been studying across the curriculum.

Activities focusing on presentation and publication

Book bonanza

Making books as a class is a wonderful activity. All the children can be involved, by contributing pieces of writing, creating illustrations for others' poems, editing the work of their peers, or actually putting the book together.

Suitable for

KS1
KS2

Aims

- To work together to produce a book of poetry based on a theme.

Resources

- Book-making equipment – plenty of paper of different sizes and colours, illustrating materials, glue etc.

What to do

1. Explain to the children that you are going to all work together to produce a class book of poetry on a theme of their choice. This theme could be a general one, such as school life, weather or animals, or it could be related to topics being studied in other areas of the curriculum, such as the Egyptians, the Tudors, or problem-solving in maths or science-related topics.

2. Talk about the different roles involved – writers of poems, illustrators, editors, book makers. Decide on a theme and give the children time to discuss their ideas and decide on roles. If it is possible to leave the activity for a few days, giving the class time to go away, think of ideas and write poems, then that would be great; you can then return to the making of the book.

3. Gradually gather in contributions for the book and make a note of any ideas the children come up with. Discuss the importance of high-quality presentation, as it is likely that visitors to the classroom will want to look through the book.

4. Spend time discussing how the book will be put together, the order of the poems, a contents page etc. Try to leave the main decisions to the children, although the younger children may need more support.

5. Allow the children to put the book together and prepare a special place where the book will be displayed. Make sure there is plenty of time in the days following the completion of the book for children to read the poems aloud or in groups or independently.

Variations

- This would be a wonderful project to involve parents in, particularly if you have families from different countries and cultures. Poems could be written in different languages, and the children and their parents could work together on dual-language examples.

Cross·curricular links

PSHE – working collaboratively is an essential life skill and can be promoted through this activity.

Other subjects can be drawn into this activity, depending on the theme chosen by the children.

Writing for a reader

Children may well write poetry purely for their own enjoyment and they may not choose to share their compositions. However, inevitably some of their writing will be read by others, and children as writers need to be aware of their readership.

Suitable for

KS1
KS2

Aims

- To present poetry suitable for a particular reader.

Resources

- High-quality paper, perhaps in different colours/textures, with borders or patterns etc.
- Writing materials (including access to computer programs that allow children to word process and use drawing tools)

What to do

1. Try to time this activity to fall at the end of a series of lessons where the children are writing their own poems. If not, and if you are wanting to focus entirely on presentation and not composition, the children could use existing favourite poems and copy them.
2. Ask the children to think about who might like to read their poems – will it be you as the teacher? Their parents/family at home? Other children from different classes? The head teacher? Why is it important to think about presentation? Does this presentation differ depending on who is going to be reading the poem? For example,

if you are preparing a poem for a young family member, you might want to make the writing very clear and large and have plenty of illustrations to engage them.

3. Give the children time to think about their intended reader(s) and to begin to consider how the poem might be presented. Discuss ideas with the whole class.

4. Show the children a piece of poetry that you have prepared for them, describing the processes you went through and how you came to make the decision to present your poem in this particular way.

5. Allow time for the children to prepare their written poem and then share with their intended readers.

Variations

• You could choose a particular theme each time you do this activity. For example, you might want the children to focus on handwriting, spelling, appropriate illustrations or setting out the poem correctly on the page. Once you have used this activity several times, the children will begin to think for themselves about the presentation of their work.

Cross-curricular links

This activity can link with most other subjects. The children need to be aware of presentation and taking pride in their written work. This activity raises their awareness of this aspect of writing.

Presenting to a wider audience

There are a great many websites where children can publish their own poetry. This is a great way of presenting to a wider audience and an opportunity for children to share their writing with peers from around the country or even the world.

Suitable for

KS1
KS2

Aims

- To prepare and publish poetry.

Resources

- Websites where it is possible for children to publish their own poems. Visit www.poetry4kids.com/modules.php?name=Web_Links&l_op=viewlink&cid=4 for a list of websites where children can publish their poems

What to do

1. Discuss ways by which we can share our poems with more people. Show the children some of the websites where children have published their own poems.
2. Discuss e-safety – the importance of not putting full names, addresses, telephone numbers or personal details on the Internet.
3. Give the children the opportunity to explore some of the websites where their peers have published poems. This would be a good opportunity to evaluate different poems. Ask them to find a page that has some relevance to topics/poetic forms they have studied at school. In this way they will feel that they are able to contribute to the site themselves.

4. As a class, explore the process of publishing online, creating a list of guidelines that all can follow (this could be done in words or as a diagram).

5. Follow the steps together and add a class poem that you have produced earlier in the year to the chosen site. Give the children the opportunity to add their own poems, having followed the necessary safety precautions and guidelines.

Variations

- Once the children are familiar with email and attachments, they could email poems to each other. It would be great fun to make up riddles and send these to friends to try to solve.

Cross-curricular links

ICT – e-safety, publishing on the Internet, email.

Appendix 1a: *Some One*

Some one came knocking
At my wee, small door;
Someone came knocking;
I'm sure-sure-sure;
I listened, I opened,
I looked to left and right,
But nought there was a stirring
In the still dark night;
Only the busy beetle
Tap-tapping in the wall,
Only from the forest
The screech-owl's call,
Only the cricket whistling
While the dewdrops fall,
So I know not who came knocking,
At all, at all, at all.

By Walter de la Mare

Appendix 1b: *Jemima*

There was a little girl who had a little curl
Right in the middle of her forehead.
When she was good, she was very, very good,
But when she was bad she was horrid.

One day she went upstairs, while her parents, unawares,
In the kitchen down below were at their meals,
And she stood upon her head, on her little truckle bed,
And she then began hurraying with her heels.

Her mother heard the noise, and thought it was the boys,
A-playing at a combat in the attic;
But when she climbed the stair and saw Jemima there,
She took and she did spank her most emphatic!

By Henry Wadsworth Longfellow

Appendix 1c: *Whoever Sausage a Thing?*

One day a boy went walking
And went into a store;
He bought a pound of sausages
And laid them on the floor.

The boy began to whistle
A merry little tune – and all the little sausages
Danced around the room.

Anon

Appendix 1d: *The Cupboard*

I know a little cupboard,
With a teeny tiny key,
And there's a jar of Lollypops
For me, me, me.

It has a little shelf, my dear,
As dark, as dark can be,
And there's a dish of Banbury Cakes
For me, me, me.

I have a small fat grandmamma,
With a very slippery knee,
And she's Keeper of the Cupboard,
With the key, key, key.

And when I'm very good, my dear,
As good as good can be,
There's Banbury Cakes, and Lollypops
For me, me, me.

By Walter de la Mare

Appendix 1e: The Witches' Spell

Act IV. Scene 1 from *Macbeth* (1606) by William Shakespeare

A dark Cave. In the middle, a Caldron boiling. Thunder.
Enter the three Witches.

1 WITCH.   Thrice the brinded cat hath mew'd.

2 WITCH.   Thrice and once, the hedge-pig whin'd.

3 WITCH.   Harpier cries:—'tis time! 'tis time!

1 WITCH.   Round about the caldron go;
In the poison'd entrails throw.—
Toad, that under cold stone,
Days and nights has thirty-one;
Swelter'd venom sleeping got,
Boil thou first i' the charmed pot!

ALL.   Double, double toil and trouble;
Fire burn, and caldron bubble.

2 WITCH.   Fillet of a fenny snake,
In the caldron boil and bake;
Eye of newt, and toe of frog,
Wool of bat, and tongue of dog,
Adder's fork, and blind-worm's sting,
Lizard's leg, and owlet's wing,—
For a charm of powerful trouble,
Like a hell-broth boil and bubble.

ALL.   Double, double toil and trouble;
Fire burn, and caldron bubble.

3 WITCH.   Scale of dragon; tooth of wolf;
Witches' mummy; maw and gulf
Of the ravin'd salt-sea shark;
Root of hemlock digg'd i' the dark;
Liver of blaspheming Jew;
Gall of goat, and slips of yew
Sliver'd in the moon's eclipse;
Nose of Turk, and Tartar's lips;
Finger of birth-strangled babe
Ditch-deliver'd by a drab,—

> Make the gruel thick and slab:
> Add thereto a tiger's chaudron,
> For the ingrediants of our caldron.

ALL.   Double, double toil and trouble;
> Fire burn, and caldron bubble.

2 WITCH.   Cool it with a baboon's blood,
> Then the charm is firm and good.

Appendix 1f: *Drake's Drum*

Drake he's in his hammock an' a thousand miles away,
(Capten, art tha sleepin' there below?)
Slung atween the round shot in Nombre Dios Bay,
An' dreamin' arl the time O' Plymouth Hoe.
Yarnder lumes the Island, yarnder lie the ships,
Wi' sailor lads a-dancing' heel-an'-toe,
An' the shore-lights flashin', an' the night-tide dashin',
He sees et arl so plainly as he saw et long ago.

Drake he was a Devon man, an' ruled the Devon seas,
(Capten, art tha' sleepin' there below?)
Roving' tho' his death fell, he went wi' heart at ease,
A' dreamin' arl the time o' Plymouth Hoe.
'Take my drum to England, hang et by the shore,
Strike et when your powder's runnin' low;
If the Dons sight Devon, I'll quit the port o' Heaven,
An' drum them up the Channel as we drumm'd them long ago.'

Drake he's in his hammock till the great Armadas come,
(Capten, art tha sleepin' there below?)
Slung atween the round shot, listenin' for the drum,
An' dreamin arl the time o' Plymouth Hoe.
Call him on the deep sea, call him up the Sound,
Call him when ye sail to meet the foe;
Where the old trade's plyin' an' the old flag flyin'
They shall find him ware an' wakin', as they found him long ago!

By Sir Henry Newbolt

Appendix 1g: *The Ballad of Inchcape Rock*

No stir in the air, no stir in the sea,
The ship was still as she could be;
Her sails from heaven received no motion;
Her keel was steady in the ocean.

Without either sign or sound of their shock,
The waves flowed over the Inchcape Rock;
So little they rose, so little they fell,
They did not move the Inchcape Bell.

The Abbot of Aberbrothok
Had placed that Bell on the Inchcape Rock;
On a buoy in the storm it floated and swung,
And over the waves its warning rung.

When the Rock was hid by the surge's swell,
The mariners heard the warning Bell;
And then they knew the perilous Rock,
And blest the Abbot of Aberbrothok.

The sun in heaven was shining gay;
All things were joyful on that day;
The sea-birds screamed as they wheeled round,
And there was joyance in their sound.

The buoy of the Inchcape Bell was seen,
A dark spot on the ocean green;
Sir Ralph the Rover walked his deck,
And he fixed his eye on the darker speck.

He felt the cheering power of spring;
It made him whistle, it made him sing:
His heart was mirthful to excess,
But the Rover's mirth was wickedness.

His eye was on the Inchcape float.
Quoth he, 'My men, put out the boat
And row me to the Inchcape Rock,
And I'll plague the Abbot of Aberbrothok.'

The boat is lowered, the boatmen row,
And to the Inchcape Rock they go;
Sir Ralph bent over from the boat,
And he cut the Bell from the Inchcape float.

Down sank the Bell with a gurgling sound;
The bubbles rose and burst around.
Quoth Sir Ralph, 'The next who comes to the Rock
Won't bless the Abbot of Aberbrothok.'

Sir Ralph the Rover sailed away;
He scoured the sea for many a day;
And now grown rich with plundered store,
He steers his course for Scotland's shore.

So thick a haze o'erspread the sky,
They cannot see the sun on high:
The wind hath blown a gale all day,
At evening it hath died away.

On the deck the Rover takes his stand;
So dark it is they see no land.
Quoth Sir Ralph, 'It will be brighter soon,
For there is the dawn of the rising moon.'

'Canst hear,' said one, 'the broken roar?
For methinks we should be near the shore.'
'Now where we are I cannot tell,
But I wish I could hear the Inchcape Bell.'

They hear no sound; the swell is strong;
Though the wind hath fallen, they drift along
Till the vessel strikes with a shivering shock:
'O Christ! it is the Inchcape Rock!'

Sir Ralph the Rover tore his hair,
He curst himself in his despair:
The waves rush in on every side,
The ship is sinking beneath the tide.

But, even in his dying fear,
One dreadful sound could the Rover hear,—
A sound as if with the Inchcape Bell
The Devil below was ringing his knell.

By Robert Southey

Appendix 1h: Falling Snow

See the pretty snowflakes
Falling from the sky;
On the wall and housetops
Soft and thick they lie.

On the window ledges,
On the branches bare;
Now how fast they gather,
Filling all the air.

Look into the garden,
Where the grass was green;
Covered by the snowflakes,
Not a blade is seen.

Now the bare black bushes
All look soft and white,
Every twig is laden,
What a pretty sight!

                    Anon

Appendix 1i: *The Rainbow*

I saw the lovely arch
Of Rainbow span the sky,
The gold sun burning
As the rain swept by.

In bright-ringed solitude
The showery foliage shone
One lovely moment,
And the Bow was gone.

By Walter De La Mare

Appendix 1j: *Futility*

Move him into the sun –
Gently its touch awoke him once,
At home, whispering of fields unsown.
Always it woke him, even in France,
Until this morning and this snow.
If anything might rouse him now
The kind old sun will know.

Think how it wakes the seeds, –
Woke, once, the clays of a cold star.
Are limbs, so dear-achieved, are sides,
Full-nerved – still warm – too hard to stir?
Was it for this the clay grew tall?
– O what made fatuous sunbeams toil
To break earth's sleep at all?

By Wilfred Owen

Appendix 1k: *Lullaby*

Hush, little baby, don't say a word,
Daddy's going to buy you a mocking bird.

If the mocking bird won't sing,
Daddy's going to buy you a diamond ring.

If the diamond ring turns to brass,
Daddy's going to buy you a looking-glass.

If the looking-glass gets broke,
Daddy's going to buy you a billy-goat.

If that billy-goat runs away,
Daddy's going to buy you another today.

Anon

Appendix 1l: *I Eat My Peas With Honey*

I eat my peas with honey,
I've done it all my life:
It makes the peas taste funny,
But it keeps them on the knife.

     Anon

Appendix 1m: *Two Little Kittens*

Two little kittens, one stormy night,
Began to quarrel, and then to fight;
One had a mouse, the other had none,
And that's the way the quarrel begun.

'I'll have that mouse,' said the biggest cat;
'You'll have that mouse? We'll see about that!'
'I will have that mouse,' said the eldest son;
'You shan't have the mouse,' said the little one.

I told you before 'twas a stormy night
When these two little kittens began to fight;
The old woman seized her sweeping broom,
And swept the two kittens right out of the room.

The ground was covered with frost and snow,
And the two little kittens had nowhere to go;
So they laid them down on the mat at the door,
While the old woman finished sweeping the floor.

Then they crept in, as quiet as mice,
All wet with the snow, and cold as ice,
For they found it was better, that stormy night,
To lie down and sleep than to quarrel and fight.

Anon

Appendix 1n: *The Way Through the Woods*

They shut the road through the woods
Seventy years ago.
Weather and rain have undone it again,
And now you would never know
There was once a road through the woods
Before they planted the trees.
It is underneath the coppice and heath,
And the thin anemones.
Only the keeper sees
That, where the ring-dove broods,
And the badgers roll at ease,
There was once a road through the woods.

Yet, if you enter the woods
Of a summer evening late,
When the night-air cools on the trout-ringed pools
Where the otter whistles his mate.
(They fear not men in the woods,
Because they see so few)
You will hear the beat of a horse's feet,
And the swish of a skirt in the dew,
Steadily cantering through
The misty solitudes,
As though they perfectly knew
The old lost road through the woods. . . .
But there is no road through the woods.

by Rudyard Kipling

Appendix 1o: *Prelude I*

The winter evening settles down
With smell of steaks in passageways.
Six o'clock.
The burnt-out ends of smoky days.
And now a gusty shower wraps
The grimy scraps
Of withered leaves about your feet
And newspapers from vacant lots;
The showers beat
On broken blinds and chimneypots,
And at the corner of the street
A lonely cab-horse steams and stamps.
And then the lighting of the lamps.

By T S Eliot

Appendix 1p: *Miracles*

Why, who makes much of a miracle?
As to me I know of nothing else but miracles,
Whether I walk the streets of Manhattan,
Or dart my sight over the roofs of houses toward the sky,
Or wade with naked feet along the beach just in the edge of the water,
Or stand under trees in the woods,
Or talk by day with any one I love, or sleep in the bed at night
with any one I love,
Or sit at table at dinner with the rest,
Or look at strangers opposite me riding in the car,
Or watch honey-bees busy around the hive of a summer forenoon,
Or animals feeding in the fields,
Or birds, or the wonderfulness of insects in the air,
Or the wonderfulness of the sundown, or of stars shining so quiet and bright,
Or the exquisite delicate thin curve of the new moon in spring;
These with the rest, one and all, are to me miracles,
The whole referring, yet each distinct and in its place.

To me every hour of the light and dark is a miracle,
Every cubic inch of space is a miracle,
Every square yard of the surface of the earth is spread with the same,
Every foot of the interior swarms with the same.
To me the sea is a continual miracle,
The fishes that swim—the rocks—the motion of the waves—the
ships with men in them,
What stranger miracles are there?

By Walt Whitman

Appendix 2: Drama and role play activities

Hot-seating

Hot-seating is a drama technique that can be used in the classroom to deepen children's understanding of character. One person goes into role and sits in the 'hot seat' and is asked questions by their peers. Questions might cover their feelings about certain aspects of the storyline (if they are a character from a book) or what their relationship is with other characters. The child in the hot seat answers as the character they are playing. It is a powerful technique that really helps children immerse themselves in a role. However, it can be quite tricky at first, and you need to model the technique several times so that children grasp the idea.

Thought-tracking

This technique is very useful for getting children to think about things from particular perspectives and to encourage them to put themselves in someone else's shoes. The best way to define thought-tracking is to give you an example. If you were reading a story or a poem about a spooky, dark wood, you might ask the children to close their eyes and imagine that they are in the wood. You would then begin to track their thoughts by saying something like: 'The night is inky black and you can barely see your hands in front of you. A light breeze whispers through the branches of the trees and there are small scuffling noises in the undergrowth. An owl hoots nearby, making you jump and freeze. A strange smell drifts towards you and you realise it is the smoky aroma of a bonfire. So you are not alone here …' You then walk around the classroom and tap someone on the shoulder and ask a question, e.g. 'How are you feeling? What can you hear?' You then continue to track their thoughts or bring them back together and discuss further.

Freeze frames

This is where individual children or groups are asked to represent characters or a scene/setting at a significant moment. The freeze frame can be improvised or planned briefly. The children need to think about body position, facial expression, their relationship to others in the group etc. so that they best represent the moment. Freeze frames work well if you stop a story/poem at a critical point and ask the children to represent what is happening or what they predict might happen next.

Conscience corridor|decision alley

This is where, following the reading of a story or poem where there has been conflict or decisions to be made, the children create two lines facing each other. One child takes on the role of a character who is facing a difficult choice/decision and walks down the corridor between the lines. The other children give their views, both for and against a particular decision or action, acting as their conscience. The child in role listens before making a decision about the course of action to take. Conscience corridor is a useful means of exploring a character's mind at a moment of crisis and of investigating the complexity of the decision he or she is facing.

Appendix 3: Emotion graphs

Some stories/poems follow a character or characters through a range of emotions. To enable children to identify and empathise with these emotions, it is useful to use an 'emotion graph'. As they read through the text, the children make a note of the various emotions experienced by a character, perhaps drawing smiley/sad/happy faces to help them remember the order. They then create a graph that shows how the emotions go up and down – perhaps starting high with a happy, carefree person; then struggling through conflict or trauma and reaching an emotional low; and then perhaps going through an exciting time (the graph line might become a zig-zag).

Appendix 4: Christmas tree template

Appendix 5: Glossary of terms

Types of poem

The **haiku** originated in Japan and is often defined as being a three-line poem with 17 syllables set in a 5–7–5 format. This tends to be the first thing that children learn about this form, and yet it is to some extent quite misleading, as the Japanese syllables are not compatible with English syllables. More appropriate would be 12 English syllables. Although it is useful for children to know this information, as well as about the history and origins of haikus, it should not dominate their thinking. Some children might want to challenge themselves to fulfil the syllabic requirement, while others may feel daunted and restricted by the format, so it is important to allow for flexibility.

A **kenning** is a compound phrase (usually two words) that describes an object metaphorically, e.g. a cat might be described as 'mouse catcher' and a chair as a 'leg saver'. Kennings originated in Old English and Norse poetry. Using kennings is a great way to introduce children to 'list' poems. Poems consisting of kennings encourage children to think about an object/animal/person and choose the best words to describe them, without completely giving the game away. Riddles are often made up of a series of kennings.

Concrete poems are more commonly known as 'shape' poems and are great fun to read and write. The idea of a concrete poem is that the layout is significant to the meaning of the poem. For example, if you were writing a poem about a very thin person, you might write a very 'thin' poem, with short words and lines that stretch more vertically than horizontally. The poem itself, therefore, becomes an image relating to the subject.

Limericks are a well-known and much enjoyed poetic form. They have a very strict structure with five lines and an 'aabba' rhyme scheme. They tend to be humorous. There can be advantages to using limericks with children, in that they provide a predictable structure upon which young writers can model their own poems. However, they are surprisingly difficult to write, because of the rules, so you need to be aware of this if you are asking children to create their own.

Most people will have had a go at an **acrostic** poem. This form is therefore an excellent starting point for young poets. An acrostic poem consists of lines of which the first words begin with a series of letters, which, when read vertically, spell another word. They can be very useful as mnemonics, where children use the poem to remember a particular word spelt out with the first letters in the lines.

Vocabulary connected with poetry

Alliteration – where related words begin with the same sound, e.g. stripey, silk socks

Antonym – a word that is the opposite of another, e.g. black, white

Ballad – a poem/song telling a story

Blank verse – poetry that does not rhyme

Calligram – where the font used to represent a poem reflects the meaning, e.g. a poem about fear might be written in a zig-zag fashion

Couplet – two lines of a poem that might rhyme or be of the same length

Free verse – poetry that does not have rhyme or a fixed pattern

Homophones – words that sound the same but have a different spelling or meaning, e.g. hare and hair

Metaphor – a word or phrase relating to one thing but applied to something else, suggesting a likeness or analogy, e.g. her temper boiled over

Narrative poem – a poem that tells a story

Onomatopoeia – a word that sounds like its meaning, e.g. sizzle, crash

Personification – where non-human objects are given human characteristics, e.g. the chair groaned as the large lady sat down

Role on the wall – an outline template of a character is drawn; words and phrases are written inside the template to describe the character of the person, and words and phrases are written outside the template to describe the outward appearance of the character. These words can then be used in children's own writing

Simile – where a subject is compared with something else to create an effect, e.g. as skinny as a rake

Synonyms – words with a very similar or the same meaning, e.g. large, big

Appendix 6: Useful poetry websites

www.poetryarchive.org/poetryarchive/home.do
www.poetryarchive.org/childrensarchive/home.do
www.fizzyfunnyfuzzy.com/
http://heatheranne.freeservers.com/childrens/PoemsChildren.htm
www.storyit.com/Classics/JustPoems/classicpoems.htm
www.poetry4kids.com/poems
www.poetrysociety.org.uk/content/membership/mempoems/memp04/
http://bussongs.com/traditional_songs.php
www.lovethepoem.com/poets/
www.poets.org/

Index of activities

Table showing all the activities in each chapter and the Key Stage they relate to

The Classroom Gems series

Ready-made ideas, activities and games to transform any lesson or classroom in an instant.

9781405873925

9781405859455

9781408220382

9781408223208

9781408228098

9781408223260

9781408223291

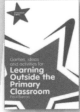

9781408225608

9781408224359

9781408225578

9781408267776

9781408267745

9781408223239

9781408225516

9781408254172

Inspirational ideas for the Classroom

Longman
is an imprint of

PEARSON

For more information visit: **www.pearson-books.com/teach**